FROM BITING
to Hugging

Understanding
Social Development
in Infants and Toddlers

Donna S. Wittmer, PhD,
and Deanna W. Clauson

Gryphon House

www.gryphonhouse.com

Copyright

Published by Gryphon House, Inc.
P. O. Box 10, Lewisville, NC 27023
800.638.0928; 877.638.7576 (fax)
www.gryphonhouse.com

Library of Congress Cataloging-in-Publication Data
The cataloging-in-publication data is registered with the Library of Congress for ISBN 978-0-87659-740-8.

Bulk Purchase

Gryphon House books are available for special premiums and sales promotions as well as for fund-raising use. Special editions or book excerpts also can be created to specifications. For details, call 800.638.0928.

Disclaimer

Gryphon House, Inc., cannot be held responsible for damage, mishap, or injury incurred during the use of or because of activities in this book. Appropriate and reasonable caution and adult supervision of children involved in activities and corresponding to the age and capability of each child involved are recommended at all times. Do not leave children unattended at any time. Observe safety and caution at all times.

Dedication

We dedicate this book to infant and toddler teachers who continuously strive to support young children's optimal social and emotional development. Your focus on children's growth, development, self-worth, prosocial skills, and attitudes about learning makes a pivotal difference in whether children thrive. Your devotion to creating experiences and environments that promote positive relationships between teachers and children and among peers will have lifelong impacts. We hope this book gives you support for your important work helping children learn how to engage in loving relationships.

Acknowledgements

We especially want to thank our family members for their continuous support and encouragement as we wrote this book. They believe in the importance of the early years and thus inspired us to devote time to this important work.

Special thanks to Stephanie Roselli, our editor at Gryphon House, who constantly supported us with her expertise. Her sensitivity to the needs of the professionals in early childhood education thoughtfully guided the organization and content of the book. We could not have completed this book without her positive encouragement and constructive support.

Donna would like to thank Deanna Clauson for her contributions to this book. Her excellent writing skills contributed greatly to the articulation of the importance of parents' and teachers' emphasis on social development of infants and toddlers with peers for their present happiness and their future social competence. Deanna is in tune with the essential knowledge that infant and toddler teachers have and aspire to learn. She also was a joy to work with on the book.

Donna would also like to acknowledge Dr. Alice Honig, who continuously motivates me to continue learning and writing about infants and toddlers. It was with her as my professor at Syracuse University that I first began to understand the critical importance of the early years. Her mentorship and friendship are invaluable to me.

Deanna would like to thank Donna Wittmer for teaching her over a lifetime the value and richness of each interaction with young children. Donna's unwavering passion for and dedication to young children is deeply inspiring. Deanna would also like to thank Nathan and Rakaia for teaching her every day how to love, learn, and grow in her own social and emotional experiences.

Table of Contents

Chapter ONE

The Many Reasons to Focus on Social
Development with Peers in the Early Years

Interaction among children is a fundamental experience during the first years of life.

—LORIS MALAGUZZI, FOUNDER OF THE REGGIO EMILIA APPROACH

Aren't infants too little to notice other infants?

What do infants learn by being together?

The toddlers in my room are always grabbing things from each other. What should I do?

I saw a toddler give a crying child a toy. How can I help toddlers do that more often?

The two-year-olds in my room are always saying, "Mine," when they are playing with a toy and another child approaches. Is this normal?

What can I do to help two-year-olds be kinder to each other?

I have a two-year-old in my room who screams when other children come close. How can I help her?

From Biting to Hugging: Understanding Social Development in Infants and Toddlers

These types of questions are common among educators of infants and toddlers. Teachers and parents of young children are witnesses every day to an incredible period of development, when children are learning at every moment about how the world around them works—and how they fit into it. Teachers know how important relationships are, and they work tirelessly to ensure that children will be good at relationships.

We know that the relationships young children have with both adults and peers are the foundation of how they see themselves and relate to others for the rest of their lives. A child's social competence—the attitude and skill to enjoy being with others and to interact successfully with others to each person's satisfaction—is central to healthy development.

What Is Social Competence?

The child:

- demonstrates a social, friendly attitude.
- jointly attends to something interesting with adults and peers.
- uses language or a communication system effectively.
- identifies emotions in herself and others.
- manages strong emotions and behavior (self-regulation).
- uses prosocial behavior, including demonstrating empathy.
- takes the perspective of others' thoughts and feelings.
- uses conflict-resolution strategies, such as problem-solving skills, effectively.

This book shares important information and meaningful strategies that parents, teachers, and other educators of children ages birth to three can use to support infants' and toddlers' healthy social development and competence with peers. We divide the ages into three periods because children differ greatly in their peer development at these times. Infants (zero to twelve months) are aware and interested in each other. We see the beginnings of their enjoyment of and challenges with peers. Young toddlers (twelve to twenty-four months) are capable of kind, helpful, comforting behaviors toward peers and often enjoy them immensely and become friends; yet, they also engage in conflicts with their peers.

Older toddlers (twenty-four to thirty-six months) grow in their ability to relate, cooperate, negotiate, and play with their peers. These developments occur when families, teachers, and programs provide the kind of care and learning opportunities that children need to develop social competence.

We know that infants and toddlers are competent learners. They thrive when they experience learning within caring relationships with adults and peers. They are social beings who need compassionate social interactions and relationships to flourish. Healthy relationships with adults are the foundation from which they venture forth to learn about themselves and others. Within secure adult-child relationships, children learn that they are worthy of love and care, affection, and respect for their capabilities. They also learn how to live and love successfully with peers from their first relationships with adults. They learn empathy and how to take the perspectives of others. They become attuned to others' needs and thoughts within parent-child and teacher-child relationships. These are challenging lessons to learn, and infants and toddlers learn them with you. They learn how to be care *givers*, not just care *receivers* (Kawakami and Takai-Kawakami, 2015).

The need for social relationships is universal. However, many factors influence how well children (and adults) learn to be socially competent. Children's characteristics and temperaments influence how others relate to them. Cultural values constantly shape their thinking and actions. Public policy and community values influence the quality of care that children receive, as well as what families and teachers think is important for them to learn.

The development of social competence is one of the most important outcomes for children's satisfaction with relationships, sense of well-being, and learning success. Infants and toddlers need us to care about their social development and learning. Let's immerse ourselves in the essential reasons why we should care deeply about infant and toddler social development with peers.

Why Focus on Infant and Toddler Peer Relationships?

So much learning happens when young children are together. Consider the following:

- Social competence creates a strong foundation for social and academic success in life.

- Infants and toddlers spend time together, and we want it to be quality time.

- Infants and toddlers are social beings. They learn from and enjoy each other.

- Peers build each other's competence, curiosity, and understanding of culture.

- Peers experience the joy of relationships—the prosocial and gleeful experiences.

- Infants and toddlers need the support of caring parents and teachers for optimal social-emotional learning.

Let's explore these reasons to focus on young children's peer development and relationships.

The Foundation for Future Social Relationships and Academic Success Is Built in the Early Years

Emotional well-being and social competence provide a strong foundation for emerging cognitive abilities, and together they are the bricks and mortar of brain architecture. The emotional and physical health, social skills, and cognitive-linguistic capacities that emerge in the early years are all important for success in school, in the workplace, and in the larger community (Center on the Developing Child, 2017c, 2017d).

We have learned an incredible amount in recent years about the importance of the first three years of children's lives. Educators and parents know that these early years are very important for brain development; infants and toddlers are learning every moment—often even when they sleep. They are developing more than a million new neural connections per second (Center on the Developing Child, 2017c, 2017d). The quality of children's social and emotional experiences greatly influences brain size and structure (Teicher and Samson, 2016). Healthy social and emotional experiences during the first three years of life enable brain growth, while stressful experiences such as persistent fear, stress, anxiety, and neglect prevent optimal brain development (National Scientific Council on the Developing Child (NSCDC), 2010, 2014). The social and emotional experiences of infants and toddlers create the foundation for their behavior, health, ability to learn, and social attitudes and skills throughout their lives (Center on the Developing Child, 2017c, 2017d).

As the NSCDC asserts in their working paper *Young Children Develop in an Environment of Relationships* (2004), ". . . the concept of school readiness is not exclusively a matter of fostering literacy and number skills but must also include the capacity to form and sustain positive relationships with educators, children, and other adults, and develop the social and emotional skills for cooperating with others."

We must pay attention now to the quality of very young children's relationships with their favorite adults and to children's social competence with peers to ensure present and later social success. We've learned that young children who have secure attachments to their special caregivers in the first three years of life have fewer behavior problems and better social competence later in life (Kochanska and Kim, 2013). We know that young children with language skills learned in early childhood are better able to control their anger and behavior as preschoolers (Roben et al., 2013). Research tells us that toddlers who feel

> The social and emotional experiences of infants and toddlers create the foundation for their behavior, health, ability to learn, and social attitudes and skills throughout their lives (Center on the Developing Child, 2017a).

inhibited are more likely than their peers who aren't inhibited to demonstrate anxiety as adolescents, but only if they are insecurely attached (Lewis-Morrarty et al., 2014). We've learned that children's acceptance and rejection by peers begins in toddlerhood and continues into the elementary years unless adults intervene (Rubin, 2002; Rubin and Coplan, 2004; Rubin, Coplan, and Bowker, 2009).

> We've learned that infants and toddlers need patient, caring, sensitive, responsive, knowledgeable, affectionate, sympathetic, language-loving adults in their lives to thrive when they are young and to eventually become adults capable of successful relationships.

Our facilitation of social development for infants and toddlers is also a key to their present and future academic success (Hymel and Ford, 2014). There is a strong link between social skills—especially self-regulation—and academic performance. Children need social competence to function well at school. Children who are aggressive, do not have empathy, and cannot control their emotions with peers are not as likely to be successful in school. Others may not want to work or play with them, and their enjoyment of school suffers.

Social competence creates opportunities for successful employment and mental health as well. We've learned that higher levels of social competence in kindergarten ("cooperates with peers without prompting," "is helpful to others," "very good at understanding feelings," and "resolves problems on own") are directly related to higher levels of education and employment and to lower levels of public assistance, crime, mental health problems, and substance abuse at age twenty-five (Jones et al., 2015).

We know more now, too, about what creates these quality experiences and what infants and toddlers need to develop well emotionally and socially. We've learned that infants and toddlers need patient, caring, sensitive, responsive, knowledgeable, affectionate, sympathetic, language-loving adults in their lives to thrive when they are young, and to eventually become adults capable of successful relationships. We know that young children need communities of caring within infant and toddler programs. We know that it is imperative that we focus on the quality of infants' and toddlers' peer experiences for their happiness and sense of well-being, both now and in the future.

Quality Time Spent Together Is Important for Very Young Children

Luciana began her group experience at three months of age in a family child-care home. She has spent most weekdays from 8:00 a.m. to 5:00 p.m. with her family child-care provider and three peers of various ages. At two years of age, Luciana, who really likes her playmates, is very sad when the oldest child moves on to kindergarten.

Infants and toddlers are experiencing their peers more often in child-care and learning groups. Children like Luciana are spending more time with their peers in programs while their parents work outside the home. In family child-care homes, center programs, Early Head Start, and kinship care (with relatives), peers share time with each other. These daily experiences support the social and emotional development of infants and toddlers—or not. Time spent together can deeply enhance—or be detrimental to—how a child learns to interact with others. We can ask thoughtfully, "What kind of peer day have the children had? What are they learning about themselves and others as they interact and relate to their special adults and peers?" We want peer time to be quality time.

Infants and Toddlers Are Social Beings

Young children learn from and enjoy each other. Social interest begins early in children's lives. Infants who are three months old will stare at another infant's face who is gazing back at them in wonder. Two older infants sitting side by side in their high chairs will gleefully laugh at each other while gently touching each other's hands and heads. A toddler will run excitedly across a room because she sees another person just her size. She will take the other child's hand in hers, and off they'll go to explore their world together. Young children often want to be with each other, especially in the presence and security of their favorite adults.

Infants and toddlers are social beings making shared discoveries. To figure out, to experiment, to enjoy, and to know—these activities are what infants and toddlers do with each other. Infants will crawl over another baby and will be surprised when their mat

> Very young children are discoverers on a voyage of peer learning in how to communicate, to make their needs known with peers, and to learn the rules of physical contact and socialization.

mate reacts with a cry. They may think that other infants are just objects and may try to taste their hair. Toddlers will imitate each other and giggle together. They will try different strategies to help and show affection to their peers. They will be creative in trying to gain access to another toddler's toy. Very young children are discoverers on a voyage of peer learning in how to communicate, to make their needs known with peers, and to learn the rules of physical contact and socialization. When we focus on these ideas, we see how curious infants and toddlers are about how their peers work.

When we see young children together, we begin to understand how meaningful peer relationships are to them. When children are developing well, they are truly social beings.

Peers Build Social Competence and Understanding of Culture

When we focus on peers in the early years, we see that through peer experiences children have opportunities to display, explore, and expand their understanding of culture. What do different peers like? Are they quiet and speak little, or are they boisterous and expansive in their language? What types of clothes and shoes do others wear? What foods do they like? Young children are learning that each peer looks and behaves differently, and yet there are similarities in how others like to be treated. They are learning about their peer culture and the broader cultural ways of others.

> "It is principally through interacting with others that children find out what the culture is about and how it conceives their view of the world."
>
> —Jerome Bruner, psychologist

As infant and toddler peers interact with each other, they also build each other's social competence. Older infants, toddlers, and two-year-olds learn to control their emotions in healthy ways when interacting with each other.

Matte hugs another toddler, Sienna—whom she likes—just a little too tightly. When Sienna protests with a loud yell and a little shove, Matte releases Sienna and hugs her gently.

Matte's desire to continue playing with her friend helps her control her strong urge to squeeze her playmate to show her affection and instead to use a more tender approach. Matte is learning about how to use self-regulation to interact successfully with her peers.

Imitation of others is an important way that infants and toddlers learn new skills and build positive relationships. As we see in the example of Tara and Danika that follows, Tara is learning from her peer how to bang a toy in synchrony and to engage her peer with a smile.

Tara, twelve months old, watches as Danika bangs her toy on the floor with vigorous whacks. Tara picks up a toy and tries to bang her toy on the floor, too. She looks at Danika with a big smile on her face.

Peers Experience the Joy of Relationships

In settings with caring adults, peers can enjoy each other's company immensely.

While Juanita, a family child-care provider, reads to four children nestled comfortably in her lap, eighteen-month-old Sarah touches eight-month-old Jacob's nose very gently. He smiles at Sarah and reaches out to touch her face. They both laugh and then turn back to focus on the interesting voice of their caregiver. In a few minutes, they repeat their playful interaction as they share pleasure at just being together and sharing touch under the watchful eyes of an understanding adult.

Toddlers enjoy being with friends and will hug, kiss, and play in special ways with their friends. Toddlers who are friends help each other, share, and play more complex games than they do with other peers who are not friends. When two-year-old Marta enters her child-care and learning program each morning with her mother or father, she looks to see if her friend is there yet. If she is not, Marta looks sad and asks, "Where Tina go?" She enthusiastically greets Tina when she arrives, and they both say goodbye easily to their parents. Tina and Marta are an important part of each other's lives. Their affection for each other has grown across the year that they have been together in their program.

When infants and toddlers laugh, show delight, and experience joy and hilarity with each other, they are demonstrating toddler glee (Løkken, 2000a, 2000b). Children's laughter and happy shrieking can echo across the playground when two friends joyously hold hands and twirl around a metal pole, chase each other across the yard, or throw leaves up in the air together.

Young Children Need Supportive, Caring Adults for Optimal Social-Emotional Learning

Adults make all the difference in how young peers relate to each other! Young children learn social attitudes and skills from the behavior of the adults around them. Secure attachments with special adults create healthy social and emotional development in children ages birth to three.

Through their relationships with special adults, infants and toddlers learn how to be in relationships. Children's ability to be compassionate with others begins early in their lives when they learn from adults who are empathetic and kind with them and who promote compassion. We highlight seven important things young children learn from you and feel with you that facilitate their social competence and development with peers.

- "If we feel safe, secure, and protected with you, we explore and learn."
- "We learn about love, kindness, affection, and caring for others—or not."
- "We learn about how worthy we are of love and attention."
- "We learn about self and other and how to take the perspectives of others."
- "We learn self-regulation, how to express and control our emotions and behavior."
- "We learn how to do the dance of reciprocity."
- "We learn social and emotional skills."

> "Social and emotional competence is rooted in the relationships that infants and toddlers experience in the early years of life."
>
> —Robin Peth-Pierce, children's mental health advocate

From Biting to Hugging: Understanding Social Development in Infants and Toddlers

If We Feel Safe, Secure, and Protected with You, We Explore and Learn

Talitha, a toddler, watched her peers play and then left her father's side to join the others as they explored the play center in the big shopping mall. She often looked back and saw her father smiling at her. At times, she toddled back to him and touched his leg, as if to gain energy for her next move into peer land. She gave another toddler a hug when her new friend had to say goodbye. Talitha's caring and trusting relationship with her dad influenced how she played with her peers.

To support and improve peer relationships, adults must first focus on their relationships with the children. When infants and toddlers experience sensitive physical caregiving, protection, and affection, they develop emotional connections with their special caring adults. When young children feel safe and emotionally secure, then parents and teachers are a secure base for them (Bowlby, 1988). They trust their familiar adults to take care of them. They are less fearful in new situations when their favorite adults are present. They know that their special adults delight in them and watch over them. They know that their adults are available, responsive to their needs, and eager to comfort and nurture them when they are distressed (Bernard et al., 2013). We say these children are experiencing secure attachments (Ainsworth et al., 1978). Secure attachments to special adults provide the foundation for optimal peer relationships.

> Secure attachments to special adults provide the foundation for optimal peer relationships.

Infants' and toddlers' secure relationships with their special adults foster exploration and learning. When adults are a secure base, older infants and toddlers will move away from their favorite caregivers and explore their environments. They know they can return to their special adults for emotional refueling (Kaplan, 1978). Children are emotionally able to engage deeply in learning and interact joyfully with peers when they trust their teachers to protect them.

Tender, tuned-in, creative, and genuinely cherishing persons help children deepen their trust in adults (Honig, 2014). Infants and toddlers who have a sense of security, or *secure attachment*, with teachers are less likely to use hostile aggression and are more likely to play in a complex way when exploring with their peers (Howes et al., 1994).

However, children who have experienced inconsistent caregiving may feel a need to stay near their caregivers much of the time. These children may experience *ambivalent attachment*. They have ambivalent feelings toward their caregiver. They want to be close but have difficulty feeling comforted by their special adult. If the adults in the lives of children who experience ambivalent attachment are uncomfortable with separation, the children may also feel that the world is dangerous and stay near adults. They don't feel safe to explore their environment and have fun with peers.

Children who have not experienced physical closeness, gentle touch, and comfortable contentment with their caregivers may hide their need for closeness and affection and avoid caregivers (Nygren et al., 2012). We say that they are experiencing *avoidant attachment* to their special caregiver. They also may avoid peers. They may hurt peers to protect themselves because they believe that peers will hurt them.

Young children must feel that you will protect them, comfort them, and be their haven. You are their emotional anchor from which they venture out for learning and enjoying peers.

We Learn About Love, Kindness, Affection, and Caring for Others—or Not

Family members and educators should not underestimate the importance of their relationships with infants and toddlers. The quality of children's adult relationships has a strong effect on the quality of the children's peer relationships. With adults who are responsive to their physical and emotional cues, infants and toddlers learn that they are good at relationships and that relationships can be enjoyable.

> "The fact is that people are good. Give people affection and security, and they will give affection and be secure in their feelings and their behavior."
>
> —Abraham Maslow, psychologist

Children who experience less than harmonious relationships with significant adults seem to experience less harmonious relationships with peers (McElwain et al., 2008). Infants and toddlers develop their initial sense of others as kind, trustworthy, helpful, and fun in the embrace—figuratively and literally—of the mother, father, caregivers, teachers, and other special adults. They learn how to be with others from you.

They learn what to expect from others. Children who have received harsh, scolding treatment do not expect others to be kind to them, either. With the guidance of adults, children learn how love feels. They learn about kindness—how it feels when others are kind to them and how to be kind to others. They learn how to show affection to others. They learn what it is like to care for others and to nurture them.

Infants and toddlers are capable of prosocial feelings and behavior. They learn, in supportive environments, to help, defend, comfort, and cooperate with their peers. A toddler with a pleasant relationship history will often look concerned when another peer is sad. And, when the toddler is able, she will try to find a way to comfort her tearful peer. Empathy and perspective taking may be the two most important feelings and skills to help children develop and to have success with peers. Parents' empathy and positive guidance strategies are predictors of toddlers' social competence with peers (Christopher et al., 2013). Children who experience empathy with special adults are more likely to develop empathy for others (Strayer and Roberts, 2004).

We Learn about How Worthy We Are of Love and Attention

Am I lovable? Am I capable? Children's sense of self that they bring to their interactions with peers begins to develop in their first relationships with significant adults. A self that is full of confidence, capable of being intimate with others, and convinced that others are likely to be enjoyable and responsive—or not—emerges from these first relationships.

Adults influence children's sense of self-worth. Children see the reflection of themselves in the eyes, faces, and voices of adults. Glaring eyes, scowling faces, and harsh words convey to children that they are worthless. Children who feel worthless have a more difficult time with peers. When caring adults delight in children, enjoy being with them, spend time with them, and show affection, children feel worthy and grow in confidence and competence with both adults and peers.

We Learn about Self and Other and How to Take Another's Perspective

From caring adults and through supported experiences, young children learn that others have different (and similar) feelings and perspectives from them. Young children develop *theory of mind*—the understanding that others may have ideas and beliefs that are different from their own—gradually throughout the first year of life. Slowly but steadily, toddlers learn that when they take a toy from a peer, that child often feels upset. They learn that when they pat gently, another child smiles. They learn what helps other children stop crying and may bring the other children's favorite toys to them to comfort them.

As young toddlers, children often prefer other children and adults who like what they do. With the help of thoughtful adults, young children gradually learn that those children and adults who like different things than they do are okay, too, and can be just as interesting. Understanding the difference between self and other is one of the most important contributors to healthy social development.

We Learn How to Control Our Emotions and Behavior

Emotional competency is a pathway to social competence (Domitrovich, Cortes, and Greenberg, 2007). When a three-year-old is emotionally competent, that child can express emotions rather than use aggression, most of the time. The emotionally competent three-year-old also understands how to "read" the emotions of others—whether that person is sad, angry, disappointed, excited, or happy—and understands how to react appropriately to another's emotions.

Emotional competence includes self-regulation. Self-regulation involves demonstrating emotional and behavioral control. When a three-year-old shows self-regulation, the child has developed some strategies for managing his strong emotions. The child might suck his thumb, stomp his feet, or use words to tell adults and peers how he feels.

A three-year-old and her one-year-old sister were taking a bath together. The older sibling, who thought that the younger sibling was being a pest, turned to her mom, who was by the tub. The older sibling exclaimed with intense negative feeling, "Ooh, I just want to hit her." Mom responded with, "You feel like hitting her, but I'm so glad that you told me rather than hitting her."

The three-year-old in the example demonstrated emotional competence and self-regulation as she expressed her feelings rather than physically hurting her younger sibling. Her emotional competence led to social competence. Children count on adults to help them control their strong emotions. If we respond to young children's anger or other negative feelings with more anger, teasing, mocking, indifference, or other negative emotions, children will use these strategies with others. If adults do not know how to help their children control their emotions, or if they think that comforting children causes them to become demanding, then a cycle of negative emotions between the parents and their children—and between their children and the children's peers—may develop (Kochanska and Kim, 2012).

Adults help children develop self-regulation. The following example of a dad with his toddler demonstrates how young children, in their relationships with adults, learn self-regulation.

Fifteen-month-old Siri runs across the inviting, long, wide-open hallway of the health-care facility, almost knocking down several adult patients. His dad, following close behind, catches up to him, takes his hand, and gently guides him back to some steps where Siri can practice going up and down, one foot up at a time.

With this simple act, his father helps Siri regulate or adjust his behavior to the surroundings. Siri begins to learn that he cannot run pell-mell through a hallway when there are many others present. Left to run without his father's guidance, Siri might quickly get out of control and bang into others as his emotions and physical activity escalate. Later, in child care, we can see his attempt to self-regulate. He runs across the room and stops himself as he skids up to another toddler who is unsteady on his feet.

Teachers help very young children learn how to self-regulate by comforting them when they are distressed and by building trust. As children grow, because they have learned to trust others, they will wait a bit for snack, trusting that it will arrive, and will be calm for naptime, trusting that their favorite teacher will help them to sleep and be there when they wake up.

We Learn How to Do the Dance of Reciprocity

Serve-and-return interactions shape brain architecture. When an infant or young child babbles, gestures, or cries and an adult responds appropriately with eye contact, words, or a hug, neural connections are built and strengthened in the child's brain that support the development of communication and social skills. Much like a lively game of tennis, volleyball, or Ping-Pong, this back-and-forth is both fun and capacity building (Center on the Developing Child, 2017e).

In an infant's first relationships, infants and their caregivers engage in a communication dance. First, the adult might lead with a smile and some kind words and then wait patiently for the infant to follow with a gaze and sounds. Then the infant might lead by making cooing sounds and the adult responds by gazing into the infant's eyes, repeating the infants' sounds, and then adding a few more sounds. The adult and infant engage in this physical and language turn-taking exchange until the infant needs a break and looks away, yawns, or becomes distressed. These synchronized dances happen many times during each day and are reciprocal interactions that involve give and take. They are mutually satisfying to both the adult and the infant. It is in these enjoyable exchanges that infants first learn how to communicate willingly and capably with others. They learn that communication enhances relationships. Infants whose parents engaged them in these responsive turn-taking interactions had better peer competence at four years of age (Hedenbro and Rydelius, 2014).

Infants and toddlers enjoy times of joint attention with their special adults. There is a sense of harmony in the relationship. Infants coo and adults coo back. Toddlers point and adults look. Toddlers babble and use words, and adults repeat the babbles, add new sounds and words, and then wait for the toddlers to babble again. It is through these responsive, reciprocal interactions that young children learn that relationships are worthwhile and that communication is a two-way street. These turn-taking chains of communication between adults and children help children engage, learn turn-taking skills, feel acknowledged, and learn to listen.

We Learn Social and Emotional Attitudes and Skills with Peers

Very young children move toward social competence with responsive, caring adults who help them. Young children have difficulty expressing their needs and wants verbally. They often use their whole body to solve problems rather than using only language. They are just learning to control their movements, express emotions in helpful ways to themselves and others, feel empathy for others, think of another's perspective, and use effective social behavior. They learn these social and emotional skills from special adults during their first three years of life.

Adults help infants and toddlers learn how to touch gently instead of pulling another child's attractive hair. They show a toddler how to pat another child who is distressed. They demonstrate how to hug gently. They help a two-year-old ask a peer for a turn with a desired toy. An adult is the social-skills guide, mentor, coach, and teacher for young children.

It is important that adults have knowledge of children's vast capacity for relationships with their peers. How adults understand this capacity affects their behavior with and approach toward the children in their care. For example, if teachers do not know that children are capable of kindness with their peers, they may not provide the type of support children need to develop these kind attitudes and actions. On the other hand, educators who see children as social

beings know that when infants and toddlers imitate others by pounding their small but mighty fists on the table, they are participating in an important social experience. They understand the learning potential of such interactions. If they know about development, educators do not become upset when these behaviors occur. They internally applaud and often even outwardly encourage these sometimes silly yet meaningful behaviors, even though at times the infant or toddler room may become noisy and the children boisterous with happy energy. With adult support, very young children build each other's social competence and experience the joy of relationships.

Children who experience conflict and feel challenged with peers need relationship support immediately. We must pay attention to children who experience conflict or other peer challenges, as intervention is most effective at an early age. Because social experiences are such a crucial part of the human experience, there are consequences for children who are not successful with social relationships. Children who are not liked or who are rejected, isolated, or fearful in social situations are usually very unhappy (Rubin, 2004). Peer rejection can begin early and has devastating effects on children's mental health.

The life challenges that children feel are often made visible with their peers. Peer relationships provide a window into the relationship experiences of a child.

Twila's experience at home was traumatic, and she was now in a foster home. At fifteen months of age in her Early Head Start program, Twila lashed out at her peers and tried to scratch them in the face if they came near her. Sometimes she angrily sought them out, only to try to hurt them or push them away. In her short life, she had learned that she must protect herself from others. While she may have wanted to approach others, she had learned that she cannot trust them—even those her size—not to hurt her. She had learned that she must always be ready to defend herself. Her peer behavior tells us how vulnerable Twila felt at an early age.

Very young children may feel grief and despair, which can cause them to withdraw from peers. They may feel fearful, angry, and aggressive with their peers. They may seem to have no interest in peers. They may use strategies that harm themselves and others. Educators may ask families to remove the child from a program. These children who feel sad, fearful, or angry are especially challenging to educators, but we must remember that the children themselves feel challenged. Adults need sensitive understanding, empathy, and a mountain of relationship-building strategies to support these challenged and challenging children. Adults have the opportunity with infants and toddlers to make a difference in their lives (and their families' lives) that lasts a lifetime.

Children Need Programs That Are Caring Communities

While attachments to their parents are primary, young children can also benefit significantly from relationships with other responsive caregivers both within and outside the family. That said, frequent disruptions in care and high staff turnover and poor-quality interactions in early childhood program settings can undermine children's ability to establish secure expectations about whether and how their needs will be met (Center on the Developing Child, 2017d).

In care and learning programs and family child-care homes, infants and toddlers are part of communities. Communities of caring are relationship-based programs where nurturing caregivers meet the needs of infants and toddlers for trusting relationships, a sense of belonging, and developmentally effective learning opportunities. Educators' relationships with families, an important part of a program that focuses on relationships, also provide a framework of support for peer interactions. A caring community makes healthy relationships the main concern of the program, from the moment-to-moment teacher-child and peer interactions to the attention given to families, the structure of the day and program, and the support that programs give caring educators (Shin, 2015).

Positive, responsive caregiver behavior was the feature of child care most consistently associated with positive, skilled peer interaction in child care (NICHD, 2001).

In programs for children ages birth to three years, a community of caring makes children's emotional and social development a priority. Caring educators know that social and emotional development provides the foundation for learning. If young children have healthy emotional and social growth, they feel well and they learn well. If they feel safe and secure, they can focus on play and peers. On the other hand, if they feel sad, angry, and stressed much of the time, they are less likely to develop social or learning competence. Sometimes teachers fear that if they are emotionally available, responsive, and empathetic with young children, those children will become spoiled or overly demanding. The truth is quite the opposite. If teachers are not responsive, they may harden children's hearts to their own and others' feelings. Children who do not have emotionally responsive adults in their lives can become demanding or can withdraw from relationships.

Educators, family members, and other infant-toddler professionals make a difference in the lives of children who spend much of their time in groups. They can create personal relationships and physical environments that help young children thrive as individuals within social relationships. We can create relationship-based communities with primary care and continuity-of-care practices (Ebbeck et al., 2015; Kim, 2010). When there are multiple teachers in a room in a center, infants and toddlers may have difficulty forming a secure attachment with one adult. A *primary-care approach* supports a special relationship between a small group of children and a teacher. A teacher is assigned to be the primary person to create secure attachments with the children by feeding, rocking and diapering the children and by communicating with the family members whenever possible.

[With primary care] all caregivers establish a close bond with their infants and toddlers by being emotionally available and spending quality time during play and storytelling activities, calling the infant or toddler by name, talking to them, touching and hugging, and providing undivided attention to them (Ebbeck et al., 2015).

With primary care, young children thrive because they are known by their primary caregiver—their individual traits, interests, and dislikes. The children feel safe with their primary caregiver and do not have to struggle to be understood. They have a secure base to go to when they are distressed or need emotional care (Ebbeck et al., 2015). This reduces their stress levels. The teacher knows each child well, including the meaning of the child's facial expressions, vocalizations, and movements. The primary teacher becomes an interpreter of the children's needs. Families benefit because they receive consistent information and learn to trust their child's primary teacher.

It isn't always possible for children to be cared for by their primary caregiver, so children need to feel safe and comfortable with all the teachers in a center's room. A primary-caregiver system in a center program adds an additional level of quality and emotional-social enrichment with an emphasis on adult-child secure attachment relationships.

With *continuity of care*, children and their teachers remain together for more than one year, ideally for the first three years. Continuity of care works well in programs where all the teachers provide sensitive, responsive care and interesting learning experiences. While having a disengaged teacher move up with a group of children would not be desirable, having a responsive, loving teacher move up with them would provide the support that young children need.

In her article "Molding to the Children: Primary Caregiving and Continuity of Care," author Rachel Theilheimer asserts that the caregivers know the children in their group so well that they can shape their responses to the needs of the children. This results in children who are securely attached to their primary caregivers (Honig, 2014). The children know each other well, too. Friendships are more likely to develop, and play is more complex when groups of children stay together for more than a year. Also, infants and toddlers experience less stress when they have fewer transitions to experience (Cryer et al., 2005).

In Swedish preschool curriculum documents regarding children from eighteen months to five years of age, professionals state, "The preschool should encourage and strengthen the child's compassion and empathy of others" (Lillvist, 2005). When programs focus on teachers' compassion for children and children's compassion for others, we can only imagine how safe and loving such an environment might feel to each child.

Young children's social development predicts and is the product of a humane, compassionate community that cares for the quality of life that children experience together. In a responsive program, relationships—teacher-parent, teacher-child, and child-child—are the key to children's emotional, social, and physical health.

• • •

There are many reasons why it is important to focus on young children's social development with peers. Infants and toddlers spend time together. We want this time to be quality time full of learning and enjoyment. Young children are social beings. They are capable of kind, loving behaviors with each other. They become friends much earlier than many have thought.

Adults make a difference in helping children feel safe and secure so that the children explore and learn with peers. With guiding adults, infants and toddlers learn that relationships are worthwhile, feel that they are good at "doing" relationships, and develop the skills necessary for social competence. Adults are the ones who help children manage negative emotions and experience positive ones. Adults thoughtfully support and encourage peer possibilities, interactions, and relationships. Teachers organize environments and plan activities with relationships as a priority. They promote children's well-being and peer relationships by reducing stress and by giving these very young children the gift of their attention, affection, comfort, and encouragement within the context of a relationship-based program.

Educators and other adults have a powerful role in helping young children feel effective at getting their needs met, learning that others have feelings, and knowing that those feelings matter. Teachers and families experience the joy of helping young children feel their connection with humanity and learn the value of social relationships.

Chapter TWO

So Much More than Parallel Play: Foundations of Infant and Toddler Relationships

So much social development and learning happens from birth to three that it is a challenge to capture the wonder of it all. Infants' and toddlers' peer social competence grows exponentially during their first three years. During this time, children demonstrate remarkable growth in their ability to interact, develop relationships, and function in a group setting (Kawakami and Takai-Kawakami, 2015; Nichols, Svetlova, and Brownell, 2015; Ross, Friedman, and Field, 2015). With adult support, children are motivated to communicate in a variety of ways, share meaning, play reciprocal games, begin to help, show empathy, defend others, cooperate, and negotiate conflicts.

Infants and toddlers develop in memory, movement, and mastery, which in turn influence their peer abilities. Their goal-oriented desires, which both enhance and interfere with peer interactions, grow each day. They begin imitating each other quite early to learn from and connect with each other. They explore cause and effect with a poke or a squeal to make a peer cry out or laugh. They play follow-the-leader games. Peer interactions become more complex as their language and ability to communicate develops. They begin to understand possession. They learn that their behavior influences others and that others can feel and want things differently than they do. They learn to cooperate and become friends with peers if caring and emotionally available adults are present.

In the past, researchers described peer interactions in the early years as solitary or parallel (Parten, 1932). In *solitary play*, each child plays alone; in *parallel play*, children play side by side but do not seem to be aware of each other. If we think of young children as only capable of solitary or parallel play, we miss seeing a whole world of peer interest, learning, capabilities, possibilities, and joy. While we do see parallel play among young children, their interactions are much more interesting and complex than the term *parallel play* implies.

We know that children's peer skills grow because of biological development. Three other perspectives illustrate how infants and toddlers develop and learn: the constructivist view, the relationship-based model, and the sociocultural model.

The constructivist view says that learning is an ongoing process of building knowledge through experience. As a child experiences something new, he will compare the new knowledge to what he already knows and develop new ideas from the new information. In a constructivist view of learning, infants and toddlers are learning constantly in their first peer relationships. Their social interactions help them to construct ideas about how peers work, how to communicate, and how to make a friend. Caring adults provide many opportunities for peers to interact (Piaget, 1952). When adults model prosocial behavior that children emulate, children construct a positive understanding of relationships.

A relationship-based model also explains how infants and toddlers learn how to interact with their peers. The relationships that young children have experienced with adults influence how children will develop relationships with peers (Hinde, 1992). These very young children also learn from their experiences with peers. Children develop different types of relationships with different peers based on their experiences. They may seek out and become friends with some, and others they learn to avoid.

In a sociocultural model, we understand that culture, family members, educators, and skilled peers play important roles in children's social development (Vygotsky, 1987). Adults teach and model for young children their cultural values concerning social attitudes and skills. Adults *scaffold*—support and encourage— young children's peer learning through observing and helping children understand how to interact successfully with peers. Adults support harmonious peer interactions and relationships through responsive and developmentally effective environments and programs.

In this chapter, we think about how all young children show interest in peers, communicate with them, imitate them, and share meaning. These are foundational social attitudes and skills not only for social competence with peers in these early years but also for relationships the rest of their lives. Throughout the chapter, you will find a multitude of ideas you can use to encourage and support peer competence and enjoyment.

Peer Interactions Are Dynamic

Peers generally want to play with each other. Their behavior is often lively, energetic, and forceful. We say it is dynamic because, in addition to being lively, it is self-motivated: Peers want to interact with each other. It is also dynamic because it is action packed with one peer's behavior influencing another peer's behavior and vice-versa. The physical and verbal exchanges we see between peers cascade interactions into relationships.

They Have Goals with Peers

Sara crawled over to Sam, reached out, and pulled his hair. What were her goals? What was she trying to achieve? Through observation, an adult might guess that Sara saw something interesting about Sam's hair and wanted to see what it was. Depending on her age, she may have been trying a strategy to get Sam's attention. An astute parent or teacher will show Sara other ways that might be more successful in gaining Sam's agreeable attention.

As infants develop into toddlers they become increasingly task oriented and want to "make something happen" or "make something work." Toddlers observe the results of, correct, and control their activities. They increasingly react to the outcomes with happiness and satisfaction as if to say, "I did it." This goal-oriented behavior with toys and objects transfers to peers. They try to make a peer laugh. They point to draw a peer's attention to a bug in the grass. They pound their fists on the table in hopes that their peers will do the same. A two-year-old might even distract a peer's attention so that he can snatch a shovel the peer was using in the sandbox.

They Share Meaning with Each Other

Behavior has meaning to very young children that adults may not immediately understand. Hitting among two-year-olds is an example of shared meaning. From an adult perspective, it is unacceptable for a child to hit another child. Yet, within one observed group of toddlers, different types of hits had different, shared meanings. Table 1 lists the types of hits, their likely meanings, and their typical results.

Table 1: Types of Toddler Hits, Their Meanings, and Results

Type of Hit	Meaning of Hit	Result of the Hit with Peer
Open hit: a low-intensity hit or swipe at the torso or limb	"Hey, leave me alone."	No further interaction
Hitting with an object in the hand such as a stuffed toy: a low-intensity hit or swipe to any part of the body	"Hey, wanna play?"	Positive or neutral interaction
Hard hit or any hit to the head	"Bam! I don't like that."	Negative interaction

Brownlee, John, and Roger Bakeman. 1981. "Hitting in Toddler-Peer Interaction." *Child Development* 52(3): 1076–1079.

Most adults respond negatively to peers hitting each other, but if they look more closely they will begin to understand how the toddlers interpret other toddlers' behavior—their shared meaning. Adults can respect the meaning of hits to the children while also supporting the toddlers in learning the words or sign language for *mine, no,* or "I don't like that" rather than hitting.

Two-year-olds seem to understand these shared, nonverbal meanings better than one-year-olds and three-year-olds. One-year-olds may not be mature enough, and three-year-olds may respond better to language than to gestures.

What other meanings can young children share? Researchers Jeffrey Brenner and Edward Mueller looked at toddlers' peer relations. They observed toddlers ranging in age from twelve to eighteen months in pairs in playgroups. After observing the pairs for more than twelve hundred minutes, they identified twelve shared themes that both children in the pair interaction understood in their play with each other. Table 2 describes these themes or shared meanings.

Table 2: Twelve Toddler Interaction Themes

Theme	Observed Interaction
Vocal prosocial	The children talk with each other, even though their messages may not be composed of words.
Positive affect as a meaning sharer	The children use laughter to indicate understanding of each other's actions. They encourage each other to repeat their performances by laughing and/or smiling.
Vocal copy	The children copy each other's vocalizations.
Motor copy	The children copy each other's specific motor actions.
Curtain running	The children engage in mutual curtain running, in which each child both runs in turn through a curtain and acknowledges the other's runs by stopping and watching and/or by positive affect (laughing, smiling, and so on).
Run-chase (or run-follow)	The children run after one another. They both indicate that this is an enjoyable and social interaction by laughing, screeching happily, or looking back over their shoulders.
Peekaboo	One child hides and appears suddenly, and the other acknowledges this by smiling or laughing. The acknowledging child may or may not hide himself.
Object exchange	The children exchange an object, utilizing the behaviors of *offer* and *receive*.
Object-possession struggle	The children struggle over possession of an object. This is recognized both by the attempts of each to get or keep the object and by their acknowledgment that the other wants it; for example, mad face or vocal protest.
Aggression	The children fight with each other and/or seek to do harm to each other, using such behavior as hitting, kicking, or hitting with an object.
Rough-and-tumble play	The children engage in rough-and-tumble play, with acts such as tickling or backing into and pushing away (all involving direct physical contact). They both acknowledge the play with smiles and shrieks.
Shared reference	The children name or label an object or set of objects as indicated by mutual pointing and vocalizing.

Brenner, Jeffrey, and Edward Mueller. 1982. "Shared Meaning in Boy Toddlers' Peer Relations." *Child Development* 53(2): 380–391.

Another shared meaning that we have observed among toddlers is affection. We have seen two toddlers touch noses, smile, and pat each other with warmth and friendliness while listening to their special adult read a story or at other such times.

Sharing a dance or a game of peekaboo or running through a curtain may, at first glance, seem to be dancing, peeking, and running, but toddlers are engaged in much more: relationship building through shared meaning.

They Play with Peers in Different Ways Based on Their Experience with Them

Evan and Matias played together often because their parents were friends. Evan frequently took toys from Matias as he played with him. Matias learned, when he was with Evan, to tightly grasp his toys. He actually preferred to play by himself.

How children relate to specific peers depends on the experiences and relationship that they have together. We say these interactions are *relational* because they depend on the quality of the relationship between two peers. Matias plays differently when he is with peers who grab less than Evan does.

Children learn to enjoy each other, communicate with each other in many ways, share joint attention (focus on the same thing at the same time), imitate to learn from and relate to peers, and play in ever more complex ways. Development in these areas is the basis for learning essential prosocial attitudes and skills, conflict-resolution skills, and the ability to manage challenging feelings. All of these pieces together are what allow peer relationships to blossom.

Development and Learning

When we interact with young children, we see that they progress in social abilities as they develop and learn in the first three years. We want to understand and celebrate the potential for children at each of the following ages: infants, younger toddlers, and older toddlers. However, there are always individual differences in how young children develop and learn. It is important to observe each child carefully for his particular social development, learning strategies, interests, needs, strengths, and goals—rather than to focus solely on the child's age—to understand how to support each individual child's learning.

Infants

Infants relate to peers in many ways. Infants are social beings who can enjoy each other and are very curious about how other children—especially other infants—are behaving.

Two infants, placed close together on a blanket, accidentally touch hands across the space between them. One turns her head to what her hand has touched. The other cannot turn to see where her own body ends and the other child's body begins.

An infant experiences another child lying beside him through all his senses. He sees the peer and feels him. He might try to taste him if he is close enough. If he hears his peer cry, he might become distressed himself. He is just beginning to learn the difference between himself and others.

A baby on her tummy, placed on a Boppy pillow with her head and arms peeking over, can view the child slightly below her on the floor. She reaches out to touch the baby boy, sensing a person separate from herself. She laughs when the baby boy laughs and frowns when she can't quite reach the other infant.

This child is aware of the other infant below her. At other times, however, it is as if infants do not notice the difference between other babies and objects. If another child holds a toy, both the toy and the hand of the other child seem to be a part of one object. A child might use a peer for his own means—for example, turning over—by grabbing the other child's clothes. Infants are learning the differences among self, other, and objects.

They Find Peers Fascinating

We have all seen young children find each other fascinating. An infant sees another infant just his size, and his face brightens with interest. Young children seem to be determining whether the other person is "like me" or "unlike me" (Melzoff, 2011).

In one experiment, six-month-old infants banged their arms, smiled, vocalized, and looked more to show their preference for still photos of six-month-olds rather than nine- or twelve-month-olds. Nine-month-olds showed their preference for both still photos and videos of babies their own age, rather than six- or twelve-month-olds. They also seemed to prefer babies who looked like them, rather than younger babies with characteristics that were more babyish. Infants, it seems, recognize other infants whose faces and movements are like themselves (Sanefuji, Ohgami, and Hashiya, 2006).

In care and learning programs, infants watch the faces and movements of other children with interest. One eight-month-old infant we observed sat on the edge of a large piece of paper, kicked her feet, and with great attention watched an older infant try to paint.

The ability to enjoy each other grows during this age period. Older infants initiate (Selby and Bradley, 2003) and coo to each other (Porter, 2003). Creepers (children who can scoot on the belly) and crawlers (children who can move on hands and knees) often use creative ways to move across a space toward a peer. They laugh delightedly at each other's actions.

Eight-month-old Peter sat and laughed at the antics of eleven-month-old Nathan. Soon both boys were responding to each other with joyful belly laughs. These infants were clearly delighting in each other (Porter, 2003).

They Detect Emotions

Researchers Mariana Vaillant-Molina, Lorraine Bahrick, and Ross Flom (2013) studied infants' perceptions of the expressions of other infants. They wanted to learn whether young infants could interpret facial expressions as either positive (happy, joyful) or negative (angry, frustrated). In the study, five-month-old infants looked at two faces on a screen. One face had a positive emotional expression, and the other had a negative expression. The researchers then played audio of an infant making either positive or negative sounds. Remarkably, when the infants heard a positive sound, they looked at the positive face. When the infants heard a negative sound, they looked at the negative face. Infants are beginning to match facial expressions with the sounds that reflect emotion (Vaillant-Molina, Bahrick, and Flom, 2013).

They Communicate, Share Joint Attention, and Relate

Benjamin Bradley and Jane Selby studied babies' relational capacity by asking how they communicate with each other. The researchers brought babies ages six to ten months into a room in groups of three, with the children facing each other while sitting in strollers. Parents left the room and returned if their babies became upset. Each baby could interact with the other two babies at the same time, for example, by toe touching with both simultaneously. One infant squealed and then looked to one baby and then the other as if to include them both. Infants found ways to keep another's attention by smiling and by using gestures including pointing at each other, frequent vocalizing, and playing "footsie" (Bradley and Selby, 2004; Bradley and Smithson, 2017; Selby and Bradley, 2003).

One child, Mona, preferred interacting with Joe rather than Ann. Mona withdrew her foot from Ann after Ann tried to engage in toe touching. Then, when Joe turned and smiled at Ann, Mona began to cry while watching Joe "desert" her. Another child, who looked often to the door to see where her mother had gone, held her own toe, seemingly to hold herself together. She spent more time looking at the other children when she was holding her own toe than when she was not. The authors conclude that there were many ways that the babies communicated with each other (both to engage and withdraw from others) and that there were powerful feelings circulating in the group.

By one year, older infants communicate with each other in many ways. They watch other infants and follow their gaze (Shin, 2012). They've learned that peers look at interesting actions or objects. They then crawl or walk to the object of attention. They experience joint attention when both children focus on another child or a toy. They point as if to say, "Look at that," or "What is that?" or "Give me that" (Brownell et al., 2006; Shin, 2012). The infants are understanding each other's intentions. They smile at each other as if to say, "You understood me." Infants' ability to engage in joint attention at twelve months predicted their social competence at thirty months (Van Hecke et al., 2007).

The following is an example of joint attention, understanding each other's intentions, and the power of smiles.

Ten-month-old Alia is sitting on the floor and playing with a plastic toy train. Nine-month-old Kevin crawls to Alia, then he looks at the toy and Alia in turn. Kevin picks up the toy train. Alia looks at Kevin, gets up, and walks over to the big green ball. Alia starts banging the ball. Kevin stops playing with the train. Kevin looks at Alia playing with the green ball. Kevin smiles at Alia when Alia looks at Kevin. Then, Kevin scoots over to Alia. Alia and Kevin bang the ball together, giggling (Shin, 2012).

Toys are interesting, but the actions that other children do with them are more interesting. In this example, the green ball attracted Alia's interest. But, it was Alia's action on the toy that really made Kevin smile. Sometimes, however, toys themselves are the catalysts for social interaction.

Toys Are the Incentive for Interaction

An infant's eyes may focus on the toy in another infant's hand, and the first infant may try to touch the toy. While some adults might try to stop the approach of one infant toward another, there are many positive aspects of a one-year-old touching an object that a peer holds. Rather than interrupting the infants, think about how they are now close to each other, increasing the chances that they will look not only at the toy but also at each other. They may become interested in each other—the beginnings of a relationship. This view of toy touching reminds us to think about the children's possible intentions from the children's perspective.

By the end of the first year, infants want to engage with their peers through toys. They hold up toys to show their peers. They may develop relationships as they look into a mirror together with peers. Toys can be the catalyst for interaction.

Young Toddlers

In this stage, increased mobility leads to much more interaction with peers. The ability to crawl fast, pull to stand, walk, run, and pull toys opens their worlds. Toddlers can be with their peers in a different way.

They Communicate in Many Ways

Toddlers can communicate in an astonishing number of ways. Most often, however, they communicate nonverbally in "silence and movement" (Kultti, 2015). Toddlers "make 'music' together, playfully composing a 'we' through frolicking moods . . ." (Løkken, 2000a).

They converse through moving and action. A peer conversation may be a series of glances or kinesthetic dance. Toddlers have a toddling style—a social style that includes running, jumping, trampling, twisting, bouncing, romping, shouting, head shaking, falling ostentatiously, and laughing ostentatiously (Løkken, 2000b).

Children in this age group begin to play out social sequences, games, and routines. Two fourteen-month-olds, for example, were observed playing a game of "lick the paper." One would lick a piece of paper and then pass it to the other to lick. They continued back and forth like this until one of the pair decided not to lick on his turn, which displeased his partner (Løkken, 2000b). They continued changing up the game in small ways and responding to the other's positive or negative physical communication. Løkken emphasizes that ". . . the children's actions showed that they tried to understand and adapt to each other's actions." Becoming friends does not always require licking a piece of paper, but in this case, it certainly enhanced the relationship.

Researcher Phyllis Porter (2003) captured some delightful peer interactions among infants of twelve to eighteen months of age in a child care and learning program. Their communications were largely through movement. By twelve months, infants interacted in play, initiated games, and instigated the action. When walking, hands became free and they offered each other toys and food. They even tried to feed bottles to younger ones. Their increased mobility and helpfulness further enhanced socialization. A thirteen-month-old girl assumed the role of leader with a group of eight-, eleven-, and thirteen-month-old children. She offered toys and food to them. A fourteen-month-old child played peekaboo under the double-decker combination playpen/maze. She enticed other children to play with her. Toddlers often cared for each other. One child put pacifiers into the mouths of younger, fussing infants. Other toddlers offered favorite blankets or transition objects to their owners to soothe their crying.

Young toddlers communicate with facial expressions and gestures. They are learning how to play with each other and become friends. In classic research conducted more than thirty years ago, Montagner (reported by Pines, 1984) observed the many communication styles of toddlers. They may soothe, calm, show affection, invite other toddlers to play by tilting their heads to one side, offer toys, and make noises with each other. They may threaten other children with frowns, fists, clenched teeth, raising their arms, or leaning their heads forward. They may use more hurtful behaviors with peers, such as hitting, biting, scratching, pinching, or grabbing a toy. They may show fear by protecting their faces with bent arms, moving their heads backward, crying, or running away. They may communicate their isolation by sucking their thumbs or a blanket, moving away from their peers, or crying alone.

Children who emerge as peer leaders use many of the affectionate and soothing techniques, and they defend themselves with threatening behavior only when necessary. Young children also learn to avoid the children who frequently use hurtful behaviors. As we focus on young children's nonverbal cues to each other, we begin to understand their remarkable ability to communicate their desires, fears, and goals. Moving together, running and chasing, playing peekaboo, exchanging materials, and imitating are powerful ways that young children relate to each other (Howard et al., 2015; Over and Carpenter, 2012).

Young toddlers relate through watching and silence. When they aren't moving, they may be watching. We may think that a toddler observing others is fearful of joining peer play. We may think that the toddler is tired and wants to refuel by the teacher for a while. These may be true; however, peers' purposeful watching is necessary for relationship foundation and formation (Davis and Degotardi, 2015). Toddlers watch their peers to learn about the activities of others. They watch because they are interested in others. They watch to participate in a shared activity. They watch first and then imitate others to join in the play of a group (Davis et al., 2015). Watching peers, then, is an important strategy that children use to learn how to relate with others, gain play skills, and respect others' play before joining in the activity (Kultti, 2015).

They Imitate—The Sincerest Form of Relating

Imitation begins just after birth, when infants imitate an adult who sticks out her tongue and waits for the infant to respond. During the first year, infants often take interaction turns with adults, with the adult imitating the baby and the baby imitating the adult. It is during the second and third year of life, however, when children imitate adults in more complex ways and begin imitating their peers in interesting ways.

You may wonder, for example, why eighteen-month-old Charlie suddenly begins to hit other toddlers. Then, you remember that Charlie observed very carefully when Gabe hit his mother when she picked him up yesterday. Charlie now can observe a peer action, store the memory, and use the same behavior the next day with a peer. Toddlers not only imitate peers, they can imitate three-step sequences. They imitate peers more than adults (in a laboratory setting), and they can remember the actions after a delay in time (Meltzoff, 2011).

One toddler claps and another does as well. One throws a ball and the other throws one, too. One tries to sit in the teacher's lap and another is right there to try it, too. Imitation is a powerful way that older infants and toddlers learn from adults and from each other. When the purpose of imitating is learning, then young children are more likely to imitate adults or more skilled peers (Zmyj and Seehagen, 2013).

One of the primary reasons that young children imitate, however, is for social reasons (Zmyj and Seehagen, 2013). Laughter erupts as a toddler chases a fly in the room and another toddler takes off after him, even repeating the first child's words, "Fly away, fly!" Through imitation children feel in tune with each other and aware of their peers' emotions; they experience reciprocity with them. What fun! Imitation is a way that toddlers communicate with each other (Trevarthen, 2001) and get the attention of a peer (Davis and Degotardi, 2015). An emotional connection develops among peers as they imitate each other's actions.

Through imitation, young children are learning important lessons about the difference between self and other. They see themselves in others as others imitate them, and they see others in themselves as they imitate others—this is called a *bidirectional bridge* (Meltzoff, 2007). Children cross this bridge many times during the day to form relationships. They learn and experiment with how others are like them or unlike them.

Imitation seems to increase until children are about two-and-a-half years old. Imitation of peers decreases as children gain a better command of language (Nadel et al., 1999). As language skills increase, children are more likely to use words to learn from and build relationships with peers.

As you observe young children, try to notice how early they are imitating each other. Also, pay attention to how they are building and reinforcing relationships through imitation.

They Say *Mine* and Learn to Say *Yours*

It is challenging to both peers and adults when children say *mine* and grasp tightly to a beloved object that they have owned since birth or have possessed for just a few minutes. Researcher Dale Hay (2006) studied how children's understanding of the difference between possession and ownership reduced aggression among toddlers. She studied sixty-six British toddlers at home with familiar peers. Those who began saying the word *mine* between eighteen and twenty-four months of age were more likely to say *yours* and to share at twenty-four months. The understanding of what *mine* means is the precursor to understanding what *yours* means and the awareness that different

people are entitled to different things (Hay, 2006). Educators can celebrate, then, when they hear older toddlers say *mine*. The children are learning advanced vocabulary and social skills!

Toddlers may distribute toys rather than give them away and may think they should have the toys back when they want them. As seen in the following example, this misunderstanding between *distributing* and *giving* can contribute to peer conflict.

> The understanding of what *mine* means is the precursor to understanding what *yours* means and the awareness that different people are entitled to different things (Hay, 2006). Educators can celebrate, then, when they hear older toddlers say *mine*. The children are learning advanced vocabulary and social skills!

Jason, after clutching three plastic bottles filled with colored water, gives them to his peers. After a few minutes, he insists on collecting them. Of course, the toddlers who now possess these coveted, colorful bottles do not want to return them. Jason begins to cry as he reaches for a bottle and turns to his teacher for help. The teacher says to Jason, "That was nice of you to share the bottles with your friends. Sharing makes your friends happy" (DaRos and Kovach, 1998).

Jason wasn't sharing. Because of his limited knowledge of the concept of *possession*, Jason truly seemed to believe that his peers would give the bottles back when he wanted them. He was distributing items to others for them to hold for a moment, but he expected them to willingly and quickly hand them back (Wittmer and Petersen, 2017). When we see the situation from Jason's perspective, we can help children solve this problem differently than we would if we think that Jason is simply not sharing. Also, helping children see the problem from other children's viewpoints leads to perspective taking—a theory-of-mind skill.

Older Toddlers

During the third year, children's cooperative play becomes more responsive to their peers' actions and desires, and they actively influence one another's behavior and goals (Brownell, Ramani, and Zerwas, 2006).

They Play in Increasingly Complex Ways

A primary way that toddlers relate to others is through play. Play is an activity that the child is not required to do and one that engages them. The purposes of peer play are many—to master the environment, to practice skills, to rid oneself of negative feelings, to learn new skills—but one of the most important purposes of social play is to create and enjoy relationships with peers.

Infants and toddlers grow in emotional, social, cognitive, and language development during play. Very young children enjoy each other while making efforts to relate and communicate. Infants need time on the floor to move and grasp, shake, rattle, and roll toys. As infants grow toward one year of age, they need play time to sit, crawl, and experiment with toys and each other. From twelve to eighteen months of age, we see *reciprocal play*, in which children take turns with each other in games of run and chase or peekaboo. By sixteen months, children engage in *cooperative pretend play*, such as taking turns pretending with a toy telephone. By thirty-six months, older toddlers use *complementary social pretend play*, in which children play different roles such as a mom, dad, dog, or baby (Howes and Matheson, 1992).

Toddlers need play time to choose materials, toys, and playmates from choices attractively displayed in the room. Peer interactions are less likely to blossom when children are herded together from one activity to another, never having the opportunity to make their own choices from an appetizing array of materials and peers. Given leisurely time to play, social interactions flourish.

> Peer interactions are less likely to blossom when children are herded together from one activity to another, never having the opportunity to make their own choices from an appetizing array of materials and peers. Given leisurely time to play, social interactions flourish.

They Use Their Words

Older toddlers also begin to use their words with each other. One or two words are full of meaning for peers. Researchers George Forman and Ellen Hall (2005b) assert that observing young children's behaviors can provide insight into their thinking. Table 3 offers some examples from their research:

Table 3: Purposes of Toddler Words

Purpose	Observed Behavior
To develop a pretend play script	"John used the word *yummy* as part of pretend script to support cooperative play with Andy."
To explain the significance of an object	"Sophia said *cooking* to tell Nicholas that the metal can was an important part of her pretend play."
To foster a sense of membership in a social group	"John's talk about his "big ball" encouraged Kaitlyn to join in the conversation by naming the material *clay*."

According to Forman and Hall (2005b), "The children strengthened their experience of group togetherness and fostered an early sense of friendship by echoing each other's talk and sound effects."

What conversations have you heard among two-year-olds? Scientist Elin E. Ødegaard (2006) wanted to know what two-year-olds talked about at mealtime. The children she observed had some deep conversations about life and feelings. One young child engaged her peers in a conversation about a scary event as she related a story about Santa Claus at the center of town by saying, "Gloomy Santa Claus was there." How do children decide who should talk? Do they know the rules of conversation? Two children in the same mealtime conversations struggled with one another over who would control a story. Almost three-year-old Ane raised her fist in the air and shouted to another child, "Me talk!" Soon the other child responded to Ane with anger, "Ah, *me* talk." This conflict between the two children at mealtime continued into their play.

Peer conversations with or without adults add greatly to children's learning. Children adapt the meaning and sentence structure of their words as their conversations continue. When adults ask thoughtful questions and make comments, a child may move from talking about the "here and now" (events and objects that are present) to the "there and then" (events and objects not present). This enhances cognitive development.

Adults learn by listening to young children's questions. By reflecting on children's words and conversations with their peers, teachers learn about children's cultures and their relationship experiences with the adults and peers in their lives. They learn about children's feelings, language skills, and experiences. It is fun and valuable to listen in on young children's conversations.

They Teach and Guide Each Other

Guided action occurs when one child manages the interaction by guiding the activities of another child through prompting, demonstration, and affective signals (nonverbal communication) in relation to a goal. One two-year-old becomes the guide in learning and informs or leads the other child in exploration. In the following example, twenty-five-month-old Bridger seems to be teaching the other children about shadows.

"There's your shadow," he says to the other children, guiding them to notice their shadows on this sunny day. Another boy asks Bridger, "Where you find your shadow?" Bridger answers, "Under your feet," pointing down to his own feet, guiding them to look down. "You're standing on it."

Guiding and teaching others is another way peers develop relationships with each other. Table 4 offers a summary of children's foundational social development and learning from birth to three years. Similar development charts will detail prosocial development and learning in chapter 3 and conflict development and learning in chapter 4. A summary chart of all development and learning potential can be found in the appendix.

Table 4: Foundational Peer Development and Learning Chart (Birth to 3)

Age	Social Development
0–4 months	• Infants like to look at each other. • By three to four months, an infant will smile at another infant. • A three-month-old infant lying on her back will reach out to touch a peer next to her.
4–8 months	• Infants like to look at, approach other infants, and initiate (Selby and Bradley, 2003). • Infants coo, smile, and laugh at each other (Porter, 2003). • At five months, infants can match a vocal expression (positive or negative) with the correct facial expression of other infants (Vaillant-Molina, Bahrick, and Flom, 2013). • Infants as young as six months of age show more interest in peer strangers than adult strangers (Brooks and Lewis, 1976). • Six-month-olds show more excitement at photos of six-month-olds than at photos of nine- and twelve-month-olds (Sanefuji, Ohgami, and Hashiya, 2006). • Infants may interact with peers with their whole body: rolling into, crawling over, licking or sucking, or sitting on them. • Seven-month-olds discriminate between angry and fearful facial expressions—and respond more to angry (Kobiella, Grossmann, Reid, and Striano, 2008).
8–12 months	• Sitting infants may poke, push, or pat another baby to see what the other infant will do. They often look very surprised at the reaction that they get. • Infants like to touch each other and crawl around and beside each other. • Nine-month-olds prefer to look at photos and movies of babies their own age (Sanefuji, Ohgami, and Hashiya, 2006). • Ten- to twelve-month-olds prefer to look at other infants of their own gender (Kujawski and Bower, 1993). • Peekaboo is a favorite game at this age, but an adult may need to start the game. • When an infant is placed together with one other infant, more frequent, complex, and intense peer interaction occurs than when an infant is with many peers. • Infants can understand another's goals and use this awareness to govern their own behavior (Brownell, Ramani, and Zerwas, 2006). • Because infants are more goal oriented than in the previous stages, they may push another infant's hand away from a toy or crawl over another baby to get a toy. • Peer-directed behaviors of one-year-olds increase dramatically. Researchers concluded that toddlers are sophisticated social beings (Kawakami and Takai-Kawakami, 2015).

Age	Social Development
12–18 months	• Toddlers may touch the object that a peer holds. This may be a positive initiation and interactive skill (Eckerman, Whatley, and McGehee, 1979).
	• Toddlers show or give a toy to another child (Porter, 2003).
	• Toddlers may point to a toy, sharing joint attention with another child (Shin, 2012).
	• Infants' ability to engage in joint attention at twelve months predicts their social competence at thirty months (Van Hecke et al., 2007).
	• Toddlers initiate play with another infant (Porter, 2003).
	• Toddlers will imitate each other at this stage—for example, often making a joyous symphony of spoons banging on the table at mealtime. They communicate with each other by imitating (Trevarthen and Aitken, 2001).
	• Actions are carried out with the intention of attaining a goal; however, goals can change from moment to moment (Jennings, 2004).
	• Toddlers communicate using their bodies (Løkken, 2000b; Porter, 2003) and in silence and movement (Kultti, 2015).
	• Children communicate in a variety of ways: actions that pacify, threatening actions, aggressive actions, gestures of fear and retreat, actions that produce isolation (Pines, 1984).
	• Infants share at least twelve themes in their play; for example, positive affect as a meaning sharer. The children use laughter to indicate understanding of each other's actions. They encourage each other to repeat their performances by laughing and/or smiling (Brenner and Mueller, 1982).
	• Toddlers are little scientists, experimenting to see how things work. This affects how they get along with peers. They are constantly doing things to other children to see what response they will get.
	• Between thirteen and fifteen months of age, children demonstrate action-based role reversals in social games such as run and chase or peekaboo displays (Howes and Matheson, 1992).
	• Children from fourteen to eighteen months old can imitate three-step sequences and imitate peers better than they imitate adults (Ryalls, Gul, and Ryalls, 2000; Zmyj, Aschersleben, Prinz, and Daum, 2012).
	• Children fourteen to eighteen months old can imitate peers both five minutes and forty-eight hours after they observe the peer (who had been taught specific actions with toys) (Hanna and Meltzoff, 1993).
	• Between sixteen and eighteen months of age, 50 percent of children engage in reciprocal play and 5 percent begin cooperative social pretend play—children enact complementary roles within social pretend play (Howes and Matheson, 1992).
	• Toddlers enjoy looking at books together by forming an informal group, one which they move in and out of, around the legs, lap, and arms of a favorite parent or teacher.
	• Toddlers love sand and water and playing with different sizes of safe bottles and balls. When each has his own bin or tub of water or sand, play goes more smoothly.

Age	Social Development
18–24 months	• Between nineteen and twenty-three months of age, 56 percent of children play complementary and reciprocal games (run and chase, peekaboo) and 6 percent engage in cooperative social pretend play (Howes and Matheson, 1992). • Toddlers may have kinesthetic conversations, learning valuable turn-taking skills, as they follow a leader in moving around the room—moving in and out of the group, taking turns as leader and follower—as if in a conversation of listening and talking (Løkken, 2000a, 2000b). • Toddlers may congregate, cluster, and herd together. When a teacher begins playing an interesting activity with one child, children often come running from the corners of the room. • Toddlers may work together constructing with blocks—for example, with one the leader and the other the follower (Porter, 2003). • Toddlers may work together toward a common goal. • Children are only beginning to understand that others have preferences different from their own and to take the perspective of another person. • Children who begin saying *mine* between eighteen and twenty-four months of age are more likely to say *yours* and to share at twenty-four months (Hay, 2006).
24–36 months	• Older toddlers share meaning. For example, types of hits have different meanings to children (Brownlee and Bakeman, 1981). • Older toddlers are becoming true social partners. The majority of twenty-seven-month-olds can cooperate to accomplish a task (Brownell, Ramani, and Zerwas, 2006). • Many older toddlers understand the difference between ownership and possession (Fasig, 2000); however, it is still difficult for them to control their urge to play with an attractive toy that another child has. • Older toddlers use a variety of words for a variety of functions, such as to describe, explain differences, foster a sense of membership in a social group, and develop a pretend play script (Forman and Hall, 2005b). • Older toddlers guide other children through prompting, demonstration, and affective signals in relation to a goal (Eckerman and Peterman, 2001).

Individual and Group Differences

Each child brings his or her individual characteristics to peer interactions. The temperament, gender, experiences, and language of children influence their peer relationships. Children with disabilities learn so much from interacting with their peers. Let's start by investigating how temperament influences peer interactions.

Temperament

One toddler wants to stay near a teacher and not venture out with peers. This toddler may need to soak up love and confidence before moving out and exploring with others his size. Another toddler runs off but checks in often by scampering quickly back and burying his head in the teacher's lap. Another beginning walker leaves the caring teacher's side for long periods of time but catches the teacher's eye as he careens back by every so often, feeling secure that his teacher is watching out for him.

Exuberant children are generally cheerful and energetic. They are often excited and excitable. If these children can control their emotions at appropriate times, they will be the center of attention. If they can't and they hug too hard, scream too loudly, or move too quickly around the room, peers may avoid them (Dennis, Hong, and Solomon, 2010). These children will need caring adults to enjoy them, share their exuberance, and help them regulate their strong emotions.

Children who feel shy/cautious or fearful may feel challenged with peer relationships. Children who feel shy are often hesitant and cautious about joining in play with others and will need adult support to help enter play. Adults may need to stay with the children until they feel comfortable. Children who are fearful often withdraw, even from peers they've known for a long time. Encourage these children to shadow you consistently until they feel comfortable and safe with the familiar adults in the room. Then, the safe adults may be able to guide the children to move, with support, into playing with peers. We will talk more about this is chapter 5.

Gender

Starting with older toddlers, boys often prefer to play with boys and girls with other girls. Gender segregation develops out of toddlers' attraction to peers who exhibit play styles that are compatible with their styles. One research study by Brenda Todd, John Berry, and Sara Thommessen found that many boys ages nine to thirty-two months prefer "active" toys such as cars, trucks, and balls, while many girls at that age prefer nurturing toys such as dolls, teddy bears, and cooking utensils (Todd, Berry, and Thommessen, 2016). The researchers found that these gender preferences in toys increased across the toddler years.

If boys and girls develop the idea that certain toys are only for boys and other toys only for girls, encourage children to play with all types of toys by displaying pictures of both boys and girls playing with many types of materials and toys. Also, choose and read books that challenge gender stereotypes by, for example, showing girls and boys playing quietly with their toys and playing actively on the playground (Wittmer and Petersen, 2017).

Culture and Language

Numerous infants and toddlers are learning two or more languages. Because interactions between infants and toddlers are mostly nonverbal, this has little effect on peer relationships at these ages. Two-year-olds will interact with each other using words from the languages they are learning. Their language is still mostly concrete—talking about what is in front of them. Children seem to figure out what it is the other children are labeling or what they want.

Peers with Disabilities

Children with identified special needs are included in programs with children who do not have disabilities. The motivation to learn from a peer is great! Place nonmobile children with their peers. Use adaptive equipment to support children's participation with others. Find ways for a child with disabilities to communicate to peers using sign language, communication boards, or words. Support a child with disabilities to start a game of Pat the Table or Give and Give Back with her peers. Toys that are attractive in the hands of a child with disabilities might entice another child to touch the object and initiate an interaction.

Encourage children without identified disabilities to spend time with children with disabilities. Comment on how children are alike rather than on how they are different: "Look, Tamara's eyes are brown, just like yours" (Wittmer and Petersen, 2017). Provide opportunities for toddlers who can pull another child in a wagon, for example. Give children time and space to interact with each other. Because teachers may be near toddlers with disabilities most of the time, peer interactions could be inhibited. Teachers can, at times, intentionally let children with disabilities interact with their peers while monitoring discreetly from somewhere nearby.

• • •

Infants and toddlers are active learners. They set goals for themselves and use a variety of strategies to accomplish their goals, which include interacting with peers. They show interest in other peers in early infancy, preferring to watch peers their own age rather than older or younger peers. Older infants laugh with each other.

As they get older, they share meaning with other children, imitate them, and begin to share reciprocal and synchronous interactions. Their play becomes more complex. They learn remarkable new skills at each stage of development on their way to becoming adept at being with their peers.

In the next chapter, we will look at ways that caregivers can support infants and toddlers in social learning.

Adult guidance is imperative to fostering the great capacity children have to form relationships with each other. Adults set the stage for children's social interactions. An understanding of early social development, empathetic observations, and responsive, proactive approaches to helping children reach social competence are the keys to setting children up for success in their relationships.

Chapter THREE

Strategies for Supporting Infant and Toddler Relationships

Adult guidance is imperative to fostering the great capacity children have to form relationships with each other. Adults set the stage for children's social interactions. An understanding of early social development, empathetic observations, and responsive, proactive approaches to helping children reach social competence are the keys to setting children up for success in their relationships.

Strategies That Make a Difference

What fun it is to watch infants and toddlers interact with each other. Their sociability is apparent. Most children try so hard to engage others. We notice the exceptions to this and strive to help children enjoy each other and learn from each other. The first strategy for supporting children's foundational social attitudes and abilities is to reflect, observe, and document children's social dispositions and abilities. The second strategy involves the essential adult-child interactions that support social learning. The third strategy includes creating a caring community by thinking about the responsive environment in the program and how the program is sensitively structured to meet the needs of infants and toddlers. The fourth strategy is to create close relationships with families. Let's start with reflecting, observing, and documenting social development.

Reflect, Observe, and Document

Observe and document peer-shared meaning, imitation, games, play, and cooperative strategies. Ask the following questions as you observe infants and toddlers.

With both infants and toddlers:
- What are the goals that they are trying to achieve with their peers?
- What strategies do they use to interact with each other?
- Do children seem to prefer specific children? How does their behavior change with different peers?

With infants:
- Do they show any interest in their peers? If so, how are they showing interest?
- Do they try to touch each other's toys? Does this seem to be an attempt to interact with the other child?
- When near each other, do they try to touch each other?
- How do infants communicate with each other?
- Do older infants seem to be able to understand other infants' intentions? For example, when an infant points, does the other child look at the object or person to which her peer is pointing?

With toddlers:
- Is there a leader who emerges among the children?
- How do they demonstrate that they know the difference between themselves and others?
- How and whom do they imitate? What is the purpose of a child's imitation? Is it to learn new skills, relate socially, or both?
- What routines, games, and shared themes emerge?
- Which children are friends? How do they show they are friends?

- What are the words that they are using with each other? What seem to be the functions of the words? What power do words have?

- How do they demonstrate that they understand possession and ownership?

- Are any children saying *mine* and *yours*?

- What contributes to toddler glee?

To answer these questions, observe, take photographs, or video the children. Share the observations and documentation with families, and discuss children's intentions. Ask families to share similar behaviors they have seen at home. Discuss the answers to the questions with team members. Create a portfolio for each child with examples of peer interest and behavior.

Use Adult-Child Relationship-Based Strategies

Adults lead the way in helping children develop healthy social relationships and social skills. Every day, children learn from the adults in their lives how to be in relationships. Scaffolding healthy social skills involves helping and supporting peer interactions and relationships without being directive or taking over the interactions (Williams et al., 2007). Relationship-based strategies can include using mind-mindedness, assuming good intentions, and encouraging and supporting peer interactions. Let's begin with a look at mind-mindedness.

Use Mind-Mindedness Strategies

Commenting on what children are feeling or thinking, just as if you were a mind reader, helps you tune into the feelings of children and helps them with peer interactions. This way of being with children is called *mind-mindedness*. As you comment on children's feelings and thinking, they feel acknowledged and learn the words to express their feelings. As you show empathy for children who are struggling, the children learn to have empathy for others. As you comment on the children's and others' thoughts and feelings, the children learn to take the perspective of others (Kirk et al., 2015).

Use rich descriptive and emotional language. Use language to describe how peers are interacting with each other, peer intentions, and peer feelings. As a toddler touches another toddler's toy, seemingly with the intent to interact, comment on these intentions. Use words for a variety of feelings expressed by children. Point out to a peer how another child feels; for example, say to a peer, "Lamont is crying. He feels sad." As children learn the names of feelings, they will be better able to express them with each other.

Encourage toddlers to use language with peers. Encourage toddlers to talk or sign to communicate with their peers. When a toddler is crying, help her say or use sign language to communicate to the peer who just stepped on her, "Please stop," or "That hurt me."

Assume Good Intentions

When teachers assume children's good intentions with peers, they are supporting children's positive peer interactions. Forman and Hall (2005a) share an example of a videative (video and narrative) called "It Takes to Give."

Carrie, a toddler, stands crying with a pacifier in her mouth. As a teacher soothes her, a peer named Lana approaches and pats the crying child on the head. As Lana's hand smoothes Carrie's hair, her hand circles around to the pacifier in Carrie's mouth. She pulls it out and immediately puts it back in Carrie's mouth. The wise teacher instantly recognizes that Lana's goal is not to upset Carrie by taking her pacifier, but rather to console Carrie by giving her the pacifier. However, Lana has to take to give. The astute teacher applauds Lana by saying, "Oh, thank you, Lana," and clapping her hands. Lana begins to clap, too, feeling good about how she has helped.

The teacher easily could have assumed that Lana was trying to upset Carrie; instead, she assumed that Carrie was trying to help. Lana learned that helping feels great!

Encourage and Support Peer Interactions

Adults who sit on the floor and make their laps available promote peer interaction as they talk or sing with several young children. Infants and toddlers come and go; they refuel emotionally by touching or plopping backward with great trust on the caregiver's lap and then are off to explore areas, activities, and friends that are farther away from the caregiver.

You can encourage social interactions in many ways. Place infants on their backs near each other so that their hands can touch. Place two infants who can roll over on their backs near each other. Observe whether they roll so they can see each other. Position two infants on their tummies on the floor in front of a long, low mirror (supervise babies carefully when they are on their stomachs). Place two sitting infants near each other with some toys in front of them or read a book to both, encouraging them to touch the pictures. You will notice that they will begin to take turns. Toddlers can eat at small tables so that they can communicate with and watch each other. Expect that someday they may break out in laughter as they watch each other shake their heads or pound on the table. Place inviting benches for two toddlers on the

playground. Create boxes lined with soft fabric for two or three toddlers, and hide them in a "secret" place in the room. This is a place where toddlers feel that they are hiding, but where teachers can easily see them and hear them giggle. They are developing relationships!

Sometimes be near—not with. It is most important that children feel safe and secure with their familiar adults. However, once children feel safe, they will benefit from spending some time with peers with a teacher near and supervising but not too close. You are an attractive partner to children, and they often will choose to interact with you over a peer. Researchers have found that, when children who are eighteen to forty months old are physically closer to peers than to teachers, the children interact more often and more positively with peers (Legendre and Munchenbach, 2011). Watch, however, for children who always want to play away from an adult, especially if their play is aggressive. These children may need support with a caring adult to control their emotions and behavior.

Build social competence. Two-year-olds who successfully enter a dramatic play scene join in the play scenario rather than try to disrupt or change the scene (Honig and Thompson, 1997). You can help children who are still learning how to successfully join in play. For example, sit or kneel by a two-year-old who wants to enter a group of other children washing rocks. Find a rock for that child to show the group as he enters, or find a small tub of water near but not intruding on the other children's play. Alternatively, ask the children whether Sam, who wants to enter the play, can dry the rocks with a special cloth you've found that is just right for "making rocks sparkle." If a teacher watches the play with the entering child, then there usually is a way for a child to be with and not against the other children.

Set up experiences that require two toddlers to cooperate, such as moving a pumpkin from outdoors to indoors or carrying water from the sink to a plant. Or, attach two safe markers to an easel to encourage cooperative circle drawing. Think about how to support children's cooperative tendencies rather than competitive actions.

Read many books about social interactions. Find cloth and board books for infants and books with large pictures for toddlers. Look for books that emphasize babies with others as well as by themselves. There is no need for formal groups in which all the young children are required to sit in a circle; required circle times often discourage children's love of books because of the teacher strategies needed to keep a large group of toddlers together sitting and listening. Rather, read books to one child or several snuggled on a couch together. Place books around the room and in a cozy corner with a comfortable space for teachers and children. Display books so that children can see the covers. A small couch for the children encourages children to sit together with a book. Provide a large couch for an adult and one child or a group to gather to hear an enthusiastic teacher read. From the time they are tiny, they can be read to many times a day.

Small photograph books just right for little hands can be filled with photos of the children in the family child-care center or room in a center. These help children learn to associate the name of a child with his photo. Create, for example, a book with the children's pictures and names based on *Brown Bear, Brown Bear, What Do You See?* "Sweet child, sweet child, who

do you see? I see Katharine looking at me." Make these photograph books available so that infants and toddlers can pick them up, carry them around, and bring them to a teacher to look at together. A photograph book filled with photos of one child from birth to three also helps that child gain a sense of self. Photograph books with photos of the children playing or just being together during different parts of the day will help create memories of social interactions as the teacher talks about the fun they have had together: "Remember when you and Jamal played in the sand table? You poured sand and filled the cups."

Using children's names and singing songs with names encourages children to notice each other and learn their peers' names—an important step toward positive social relationships. Name games are perfect for infants and toddlers; for example, sing, "Where is Sammy? Where is Sammy? Here he is." Point to him with a surprised or pleased look. Laminate large photos of each child and hold them up to an informal group who are standing or sitting near you. Ask, "Who is this?" If no one can guess (including the child whose photo it is), tell them and hold the photo near the subject's face. Use the names of the children often to point out to one child what another child is doing. For example, sit with a small group of toddlers to eat at a table, and say each child's name to greet them. When a child says goodbye for the day, encourage the other children to say goodbye to him by name.

Create a Caring Community—Environments and Responsive Program Planning

Young children have a great need for consistent and nurturing routines and interactions to support brain development. An *experience-expectable environment* in programs is "one in which teachers consistently provide positive and nurturing interactions within daily routines and activities to enhance children's learning" (La Paro and Gloeckler, 2016). With this type of care, which cherishes children and understands their needs, young children develop expectations for warm, comforting, and stimulating relationships—with both adults and their peers.

Environments

Encourage peer interactions by giving children long periods of time to explore in an organized environment stocked with a selection of materials that are age and stage appropriate. Place infants in a "nest" together, with a watchful adult close by, to support peer looking and touching. A safety mirror attached to the wall with a mat in front of it entices infants and toddlers to play with their images, imitating each other in their reflections. Create cozy corners for two, or provide a small center that is just right for several children. Other comfortable and inviting corners and play spaces can include dramatic play, a book nook, active play spaces, building spaces, a sensory area, and a creative corner. Dramatic play clothes, scarves, play stoves, dolls, and accessories invite peer discoveries. Comfortable child-size and adult couches allow older infants and toddlers to sit close to each other, look at books, and share hugs with teachers and their peers. Active play spaces invite children to use their large muscles to move, throw balls, and climb on mats together. Building areas embrace children's noisier play. Sensory areas can include rocks in a shallow container of water set on a short table. This invites four children to stand around the table, splash the water, feel the rocks, and laugh with each other. Place the table against the wall and hang a safe mirror on the wall above it, and the children will have a new peer experience.

For toddlers, larger equipment, structures, or play elements lead to fewer conflicts and aggression (DeStefano and Mueller, 1982). Common areas, such as a well-marked pretend parking lot in the block area, encourage children to use the spaces together. Everyone can park their cars in the space.

The sizes of toys seem to make a difference. Based on her studies of toddlers, researcher Gunvar Løkken (2000b) theorizes that with smaller toys, the conclusion of the children might be, "This toy is for *me* to play with," while with larger play elements children would assume, "This thing is for *us* to play with."

Toys that are open ended—blocks, dramatic play materials, art materials, water, boxes—lend themselves to more agreeable peer play. There is not one right way to play with these materials, and children with many different interests and abilities can play together more easily with them.

Responsive Program Planning

A developmentally effective program is age, individual, and culture appropriate for children in a group setting. This is a program in which teachers plan for individual children's needs, strengths, and interests. Children have long periods from which to choose activities that change based on their interests and goals. This builds children's attention and focus as they are given time to persevere at tasks. The schedule is responsive to the needs of the children in a room. The philosophy builds on the belief that children are active learners.

Freedom, time, and space to move are important. Løkken argues that it may be a right of toddlers to move freely with their peers. She emphasizes that "play supported mainly by the toddler body may be argued to be more socially meaningful to the children than play with small toys . . . the cultivation of peer relations at this age seems to be more bodily joyful than toyful. . . ." According to researcher Phyllis

Porter, *containerizing* is a barrier to social interactions. When a child is wrapped in the hard plastic of a car seat, an entertainer, or a swing, that child is hindered from experience, including peer experience (Porter, 2003).

In a responsive program environment, teachers consider children's developmental abilities. For example, toddlers have a difficult time sitting for very long in groups, but they usually join with their peers when a teacher sits on the floor and brings out her mitten with the props of a favorite story or rhyme. Most people love at least some types of music, and babies are no exception. They perk up and listen when a teacher sings a lively tune such as "Where Is Thumbkin?" They relax to a soothing song such as "Lullaby and Good Night." Small informal groups interacting like this are interesting to toddlers—if they are not too busy with other tasks.

Support Families

Children's interactions with their families are the cornerstone of their social competency. The attachment bonds between a child and her parents or other family adults are the basis of security, and a secure child is one who is free to explore, learn, and approach relationships with confidence and positivity. Parental responsiveness that leads to strong early secure attachment in young children is directly related to peer competence (Groh, 2014). As researcher Holly Brophy-Herb puts it, maternal responsiveness "provides not only a model for desirable social behaviors, but also opportunities for toddlers to learn and perhaps practice new social skills. For example, the mother who responds quickly when her toddler vocalizes during an activity by commenting to the child, smiling, or making eye contact is demonstrating what are generally considered to be socially desirable behaviors, namely reflecting empathy, interest, and kindness" (Brophy-Herb, 2011).

Help families understand that children learn directly from them how to be in relationships. When parents and family members are responsive to a child's needs and model emotional awareness, empathy, and connection, they are teaching relationship skills and attitudes and helping to build interaction competence. Having secure attachments with responsive adults can even help infants with irritable temperaments. Those babies with irritable temperaments who had secure attachments to their mothers were more sociable and more exploratory as toddlers (Stupica et al., 2011).

Encourage parents to use positive guidance strategies that include empathy for others and that label emotions with words. Teach families about the importance of talking to children. In a groundbreaking study, Craig Hart and Betty Risley (1995) discovered that children from more talkative families hear thirty million more words by the time they are three years old than do children from less talkative environments. The quality of the language differs also. Children in talkative families often hear more positive, encouraging language. When children hear and engage with family members in a talk-rich environment, they are learning a rich, extensive vocabulary. Language directed at the child—not language the child hears from TV—predicts children's language abilities (Weisleder and Fernald, 2013). How much parents engage verbally with their children predicts children's language skills (Fernald and Weisleder, 2015).

Language gives a child more tools to navigate peer interactions. Parent-child "turn-taking" interactions at nine months of age were found by researchers Monica Hedenbro and Per-Anders Rydelius to be directly correlated to higher peer competence and social competence at forty-eight months (Hedenbro and Rydelius, 2014). Parents and caring family members can support children's developing social skills. Researchers Rosie Ensor and Claire Hughes found that connected conversations between mother and child—particularly using emotion-descriptive language—resulted in higher social understanding in the children (Ensor and Hughes, 2008).

Provide resources, such as articles and videos, to help parents learn these skills of interacting with their children. Encourage families to talk with their children about their day and their relationships with their peers. Send picture books home from school with photos of the children they play with during the day. This will spark children to use the names of the other children and provide motivation to say some words about their friends.

Summary of Strategies

Adults can scaffold social competence by using language to talk about what peers are doing and feeling, encouraging toddlers to use language with their peers, modeling positive relationship behaviors, and staying close to support peer interactions. Interesting environments with cozy, well-defined areas in the room spark children's interactions with each other.

- Reflect, observe, and document:
  - » Reflect on the goals, strategies, and theories of children when interacting with peers.
  - » Observe and document peer shared meaning, imitation, games, play, and cooperative strategies.
- Use adult-child relationship-based strategies:
  - » Use mind-mindedness strategies, such as commenting on what the child is thinking and feeling, and taking the perspective of the child.
  - » Use rich descriptive and emotional language with children so that children learn words to express and understand feelings.
  - » Encourage toddlers to use verbal or sign language with peers.
  - » Help children take the perspective of others.
  - » Assume good intentions.
  - » Encourage and support peer interactions and relationship building.
  - » Sometimes be near—not with—to give peers opportunities to interact.
  - » Build social competence by helping older toddlers enter others' play, thus setting up opportunities for cooperation.
  - » Read children's books about social interactions that model helpful, kind behaviors.

- » Create photograph books of children in the room to help children learn the names of their peers.
- » Use children's names and sing name songs often so children learn peers' names.
- Create a caring community:
  - » Give children long periods of time to explore an enriched environment.
  - » Place infants in a "nest" together so they can look at and interact with each other.
  - » Place a long, low mirror on the wall with a mat in front of it. Place two babies together to look in the mirror.
  - » Place older infants' and toddlers' high chairs beside each other so infants can touch each other and laugh together.
  - » Provide older infants and toddlers clearly defined areas in the room—book nook, active play spaces, building spaces, a sensory area, and a creative corner. This encourages peer play in an area.
  - » Provide larger equipment, structures, or play elements that lead to fewer peer conflicts.
  - » Provide common areas that encourage children to use the space together.
  - » Provide open-ended materials, such as blocks, dramatic play materials, art materials, water, and sand, which accommodate peers at different skill levels playing together.
  - » Let children move freely. Do not containerize them. Peers cannot interact when placed in containers.
  - » Entice children to participate in group time, but do not force them. Enforced group times can lead to peer frustration.

- Support families:

  » Encourage families to be responsive to children's needs. Children learn many relationship attitudes and skills and build interaction competence in their relationships with family members.

  » Encourage connected turn-taking conversations between adults and infants and toddlers.

  » Encourage positive guidance strategies that include empathy for children and teaching children what to do.

  » Provide information on the importance of attachment security. It predicts peer competence.

The basic social and emotional skills needed to interact, communicate, imitate, share meaning, and play create the foundation for children to be prosocial with their peers. We turn to this next.

Chapter
FOUR

The Caring Capacities—Being Prosocial,
Hugs with Friends, and Having Fun

When we see children as capable of caring and supporting relationships with each other and we support their capacity for those relationships, they carry that self-image with them into the world (Gillespie and Hunter, 2010).

- Can toddlers really be friends with other toddlers? They seem too young to have friends.

- I saw a toddler give a crying child a toy. How can I help toddlers do that more often?

- What can I do to help both younger and older toddlers to be kinder to each other?

- I want to create a caring classroom where we all—teachers included—are nicer to each other. How do I do that?

In this chapter, we discuss how children learn to be prosocial with actions such as being kind, feeling empathy, and comforting others. We learn how familiarity with peers enhances positive interactions and how toddlers become friends. We discover how young children, with trusting abandon, experience glee with a peer. We recognize how adults hold the key to promoting and supporting children's prosocial attitudes and behavior.

After Maria gets hurt, she grabs her bunny tightly around his neck and cries a few tears. Santiago, who is sitting near her looking concerned, comments, "She sad," as he gently reaches out to touch Maria's head. "Are you okay?" asks another nearby child, Timmy. He tentatively touches her arm while seemingly also aware that Maria may need space. He looks concerned as he asks her, "What's wrong?" Santiago goes to get a sticker after commenting to the others, "Maybe she'd like a sticker." A third child, Ella, moves in closer and touches Maria gently on the head.

This example is remarkable not only for what the boys and Ella do, but also for what they don't do. They don't move in too closely, and they don't compete for Maria's attention. They seem to have her needs in mind.

When young children are prosocial, they help and comfort their peers. They show warmth and affection; share space and toys; cooperate with each other; and show empathy, compassion, and understanding of others. Many people have a hard time imagining that toddlers can be prosocial. After all, aren't they in their terrible twos? Toddlers certainly have conflicts, but they are also capable of caring for others. In fact, they have a great capacity to care.

Twenty-five-month-old Zack is bringing twenty-seven-month-old Tamara's baby doll and blanket back to her in their homeroom. Tamara had been playing with them at the end of the hallway; then she started crying and ran back to her homeroom, leaving behind her blanket and doll. Zack, with a look of determination, marches the doll and blanket up the hallway and into the room to Tamara. He doesn't seem to value the doll himself (he hangs on to it by its toes), but he behaves as if he thinks it is of value to Tamara. He strides in and immediately gives the treasures to Tamara. He seems to have Tamara in his thoughts as he intentionally delivers Tamara's prized possessions to her.

The Caring Capacity of Young Children

Why do many very young children help and comfort others? Humans are born with the desire to help and show concern for others (Hepach, Vaish, and Tomasello, 2013; Thompson and Newman, 2013; Warnekan, 2013). Children also learn to be prosocial from their interactions with others (Brownell, 2013). If children experience pleasure and gain positive attention when they help others, then they are motivated to continue to be prosocial (Paulus and Moore, 2012; Paulus, 2014). While research has found that children are intrinsically motivated to help and comfort others, research also clearly shows that adults and children's experiences play important roles in supporting young children's prosocial development.

> You nurture the peer prosocial spark in infants and toddlers with your affectionate and compassionate relationships with them.

Caring adults support infants' and toddlers' caring attitudes with peers. Children who have experienced kindness and love are more likely to be more prosocial with others and to expect others to be prosocial to them. In addition to helping infants and toddlers feel secure, parents and teachers who sensitively respond to children's distress, hunger, and needs for comfort and safety are modeling prosocial attitudes and behavior. You nurture the peer prosocial spark in infants and toddlers with your affectionate and compassionate relationships with them.

While parents have observed children's kindness for centuries, researchers began to understand young children's prosocial abilities in the late 1970s. Researchers Carolyn Zahn-Waxler, Marian Radke-Yarrow, and Robert King studied children ten months to two-and-a-half years of age, observing the children's "capacity to care" (Zahn-Waxler, Radke-Yarrow, and King, 1979). Three age groups were observed: ten to nineteen months, fifteen to twenty-four months, and twenty to twenty-nine months. For a period of nine months, mothers reported on their children's responses to others' anger, fear, sorrow, pain, or fatigue (or any other negative emotion), as well as to others' positive emotions, such as affection and pleasure. Researchers read the detailed journals parents kept and then analyzed simulated emotional incidents set up by the researchers every third week in the home. For example, the mother bumped her foot against an object and verbalized, "Ouch, my foot!" to see how her child would respond.

Prosocial behavior increased with the age of the children and took many forms. Incredibly, of the ten- to nineteen-month-olds and fifteen- to twenty-four-month-old children, 11 percent exhibited prosocial responses, such as touching, patting, or presenting comforting objects. In the twenty- to twenty-nine-month-old group, 33 percent exhibited prosocial responses. In the fifteen- to-twenty-four-month and twenty to-twenty-nine-month age groups, most of the children showed verbal sympathy, reassurance, and concern, saying things such as, "That's okay," and "You're okay now. You'll be happy." Many asked questions such as, "What's the matter?" or rubbed the person's hurt foot. Many egocentrically tried to lovingly help the victim by providing something that would comfort themselves; for example, a child offered her own bottle to her mother, lay down with her, and then proceeded to drink her own bottle. We can recognize that while the mother probably did not want to drink from the bottle, the toddler offered her something that was very precious to herself. Toddlers were, at times, also capable of thinking about what the other person might want or need—called *decentering*.

Most of the children in the two older groups helped in some way; for example, one child brought a sweater to a chilly grandmother. At other times, they had the great idea of enlisting the help of a third party—usually their mother. Almost all the oldest age group (twenty to twenty-nine months) shared at some time during the study.

While most of the children were capable of being prosocial, most toddlers in the two oldest groups used both prosocial and aggressive behaviors. A few children deliberately hurt others and, while seemingly aware of the other child's distress, continued to inflict pain and distress. Infants and toddlers have the capacity to care; however, they need adults to help them develop their caring competence.

From Biting to Hugging: Understanding Social Development in Infants and Toddlers

Prosocial Development and Learning

Early childhood educators want to help children become kind, generous, and empathic. Starting early is important, because early prosocial tendencies often continue into later years (Hyson and Taylor, 2011).

The following sections detail the vast prosocial development experienced by infants and toddlers during early childhood. When teachers and parents understand this learning process, they can effectively and enthusiastically support and enhance children's prosocial skills.

Prosocial Development in Infants

Clearly, adults should never underestimate the competence of young children . . . young babies have a remarkable capacity for prosocial behavior, an ability greatly underestimated by traditional child development theorists (McMullen et al., 2009).

Through creative research, scientists have opened our eyes to the prosocial behaviors of infants. Infants can judge whether a person is nice or not. They show their affection through cuddling, hugs, and patting their peers. They may look to adults to help a peer in need. They try to comfort their peers. Let's look at each of these in detail.

To the surprise of many, very young infants can decide which of two people is a nice person and who is a not-so-nice person—in other words, can make social judgments (Hamlin et al., 2007). In a study by Kiley Hamlin and Karen Wynn, five-month-old infants and nine-month-old infants watched as a dog puppet tried and failed to open a box. Then a cat puppet in a gray shirt (the opener) helped the dog puppet open the box. In the next scene, another cat puppet in an orange shirt (the closer) slammed the box closed even though it was clear that the dog puppet was trying to open the box. When offered the opener puppet or the closer puppet, 72 percent of five-month-olds and nine-month-olds reached for and held the helper puppet. These very young children preferred prosocial puppets over antisocial puppets. Infants can make judgments about who will help them and who will harm them (Hamlin and Wynn, 2011).

Amazingly, three-month-olds seem to be capable of making these same judgments. Infants—little beings who are largely helpless and have difficulty even grasping objects—look longer at helper puppets than at puppets that hinder another from achieving his goal (Hamlin et al., 2010). It is no wonder that infants may emotionally and physically avoid a caregiver who is harsh with them and others.

Infants can show affection. How do infants show affection to another child? Do infants snuggle, nestle, huddle, or cuddle together? They do when these behaviors are encouraged and modeled. Two infants lying on their sides facing each other may reach out and touch hands. Two infant boys may crawl toward each other with big smiles on their faces. Two crawling girls may give each other wet kisses. These affectionate interactions were observed by Mary McMullen and colleagues (2009) in three infant-toddler classrooms, where teachers were both responsive and kind and supported and encouraged peer-caring behavior.

"We try to make the children feel special and unique by providing interesting activities that are challenging but achievable for each and every one of them. We provide the support and encouragement needed for them to complete the tasks and gain a sense of pride. We put mirrors around the room so they can see themselves playing, and we communicate to them how special we think they are by giving them lots of hugs throughout the day." —teacher comment (McMullen et al., 2009).

These teachers, who were professionally trained and highly experienced, believed in the importance of relationships. They hugged and cuddled the babies often, creating a loving, warm environment where babies felt a sense of belonging and safety with their primary caregivers. The infants and young toddlers in these three rooms learned how to be prosocial with their peers in the arms of devoted adults.

Infants expect adults to help others. One of the first prosocial behaviors young children exhibit is helping. Even infants under one year of age seem to understand another's need for help. Researcher Moritz Köster and colleagues found that nine-month-olds expect adult helpers to come to the aid of a character that the little ones saw had difficulty achieving a goal rather than a character that achieved a goal on his own. Could the infants tell the helping character who needed help? No. However, when the helper character entered the scene, the silent infants looked at the character who needed help, obviously expecting the helper to assist the needy character. The infants also looked surprised if the helper came to the aid of the nonneedy character (Köster et al., 2016).

Infants develop and communicate empathy. Empathy is defined as ". . . the capacity to observe the feelings of and to respond with care and concern for that other . . ." (Quann and Wein, 2006). It also includes understanding that the feeling started with the other person rather than within ourselves. When we see or hear what another person is feeling, the same brain circuits come alive in us (Davidov et al., 2013). When another person is distressed, if we have empathy, we then show concern or try to do something for the unhappy person. In the past, we've thought that infants cannot possibly have concern for others in the first year of life. However, researchers have found that babies starting at eight months of age did show concern for their distressed mothers by their facial or vocal expressions, their seeming curiosity about the distress, and/or their attempt to comfort the mother (Roth-Hanania et al., 2011). It seems that infants can respond in ways that demonstrate empathy.

Jane Liddle and her colleagues in Australia wondered how infants would react to another baby showing distress and whether unhappy infants would be comforted by another baby's concern for them. Twenty-five seven- to ten-month-old infants were observed in groups of three, sometimes with their mothers present and sometimes without. The three babies were brought together in identical strollers and placed in a triangle. With some effort, they could touch each other. With or without their mothers' presence, infants responded to their peers' distress with gazes, frowns or smiles, waving, reaching, touching, and vocalizing. The following is an example of how Johanna and Fred helped Annie when she was upset. Notice how her peers' gazes, sounds, and swinging legs help Annie smile.

Annie is upset. Twelve seconds later, she meets the gaze of Johanna, who is watching her. Johanna returns Annie's gaze and raises the fingers of her hand in a wave. Annie pauses in her fussing and kicks her legs at Johanna. Johanna is looking at Fred and misses Annie's response. Annie resumes fussing immediately, kicks her legs, and shakes her head from side to side. Annie then turns to look at Fred, who has been watching her. They gaze mutually for three seconds before Annie looks away, no longer distressed.

Watched by Johanna, Fred calls Annie back with a vocalization and a smile. Annie briefly looks at Fred before turning away and rubbing her eyes. Fred repeats the vocalization with his legs outstretched toward Annie, looks toward Johanna, and back to Annie. Annie looks at Fred and then down at his swinging legs. As Fred swings his legs, he repeats the vocalization for the third time with a smile. Johanna vocalizes in response, and lifts her fingers in the wave gesture while looking at Fred. Annie subsequently engages in this game of leg swinging, mutual gaze, smiling, and vocalizing with Johanna and Fred, which continues for almost three minutes (Liddle et al., 2015).

In this experiment, babies didn't turn away from distressed infants. They rarely responded by becoming distressed themselves. They seemed to know the difference between themselves and others, and that it was the other baby who was unhappy, not them. Most of the responses were gazes at the distressed baby; however, some infants looked toward the crying baby's mother, as if expecting her to help her baby. Gazes at other infants who were distressed shows that babies were interested and curious about their peer's unhappiness. The young infants also responded to another infant's distress with facial expressions, waving, reaching, touching, and vocalizing approximately 50 percent of the time. Over one-third of the times that infants responded to a peer's cries, they were successful at helping the other baby become less distressed.

The experiment showed the beginnings of empathy and prosocial comforting when infants are not yet one year old. Jane Liddle and colleagues called these beginnings examples of "baby empathy."

Prosocial Development in Toddlers

When a younger infant starts to cry, a toddler in the room runs over and kisses him on the head. When fifteen-month-old Sawyer enters his toddler room one morning, two girls run to give him a hug. Toddlers pat each other as they have been gently patted when they are distressed. Prosocial behaviors occur much more during the second and third years of life.

Researchers Celine Scola, Claire Holvoet, Thomas Arciszewski, and Delphine Picard, inspired by the studies by Wynn, Hamlin, and colleagues, investigated whether young children prefer prosocial or antisocial "others." In their study, one- and two-year-olds were presented with short cartoons in which a character (the protagonist) engaged in ball play with two others. One character (the giver) acted prosocially, and the other (the keeper) behaved antisocially. Afterward, the children were presented with the giver and the keeper characters and encouraged to reach for the one they wanted. Most toddlers (77 percent) chose the giver, even if the color of the face was changed or the face was scrambled (Scola et al., 2015).

Toddlers prefer prosocial over antisocial behavior and can make social judgments. Infants and toddlers prefer positive people and avoid negative, antisocial people (Vaish et al., 2010). It makes sense for their own survival that infants and young children prefer kindness over meanness. Yet, it is surprising that they can make these judgments so early in life.

These judgments affect whom toddlers will help and imitate. Twenty-one-month-old toddlers were more likely to help reach for an out-of-reach object for an adult who, in a previous interaction, intended to (but was prevented in some way) give them a toy (Dunfield and Kuhlmeier, 2010). The toddlers not only determined the kind intentions of the researcher but also found a way to help. Toddlers also decide who to imitate based on behavior. Sixteen-month-olds chose to eat foods that prosocial puppets ate, rather than foods that antisocial puppets ate (Hamlin and Wynn, 2012). We wonder whether toddlers in a child care and learning program help and imitate only those adults and peers who are prosocial.

Toddlers help each other during play. Taking a toy to another toddler is called *instrumental help*. Toddlers also may help a friend who has been hurt or is sad. This type of helping is the more *empathic* type of help (Svetlova et al., 2010). Orly, in the following example, is helping Carly in both an instrumental and empathic way.

Carly is playing near the toy shelf when Tommy runs by, accidentally stepping on her fingers. She begins to cry. Orly stands nearby briefly and watches as a teacher comes and picks Carly up onto her lap. Orly turns, walks to the cubbies, and gets Carly's bottle and blankie. Orly takes these to Carly, hands them to her, and stands briefly until Carly stops crying so hard. Orly then returns to the book he was reading" (Whaley and Rubenstein, 1994).

Orly thought about what would help Carly stop crying, and then he found the comforting objects. Both younger and older toddlers help their peers (Hepach et al., 2016). In one laboratory observation, eighteen-month-old and thirty-month-old children helped other children who needed assistance reaching some balls to continue a game. The helping toddlers didn't keep the balls for themselves; they handed them over to their needy peers. Toddlers want to help adults, too (Hepach et al., 2013). In another experiment, eighteen-month-old children helped an adult who needed assistance accomplishing a task—whether the adult was present or not (Hepach et al., 2017).

Sometimes young children are puzzled about how to help. A toddler who saw a peer catch his hand in a drawer in a parent-child playgroup wasn't sure how to help the crying child. Finally, he placed his thumb in the crying child's mouth, which soothed the hurt child. We can look for and verbally recognize these valiant efforts of young children to help both adults and peers. In helping peers who are distressed, we see empathy displayed and developing.

A toddler looks concerned when a peer across the room begins to cry. A toddler brings a grumpy peer some toys. Another child goes to get a sticker for a friend who has hurt himself and is crying while holding his stuffed bunny tightly. These children seem to feel *empathy* for their peers: They are beginning to understand others' emotions and are trying to comfort others. To have empathy, infants and toddlers must be able to read another's emotions of distress, sadness, or frustration. The concerned eyes of children who feel empathy tell us that they are responding to the feelings of other children.

Researchers Valerie Quann and Carol Anne Wien (2006) studied empathy in infants and toddlers. They saw thirteen episodes of empathy during nine three-hour observations. Three types of empathy emerged from the observations.

- **Proximal empathy:** One child is near another who is upset. The first child did not cause the other child to be hurt or upset but still responds with care and concern for the other child's distress.

  Twenty-three-month-old Destiny and twenty-month-old Pratha play in the creative area, attempting to make scissors cut paper. Destiny, who has not had much experience using scissors, struggles to hold them. As she struggles, her index finger bends backward and she begins to cry. Pratha says, "Ouch," and touches Destiny's hand. Pratha then looks up, presumably for a teacher. Teacher Leona comes over with ice and comforts Destiny. Pratha stands near with a concerned look on her face.

- **Altruistic empathy:** A child is not near a distressed child, but stops what he is doing to try to comfort the upset child, going out of his way to help.

  Twenty-two-month-old Matthew is out of sorts today, crying at the gate of the classroom door and wanting to leave (presumably to go after his mother, who left about an hour earlier). Two teachers have tried to comfort and distract him, but he remains upset. Seventeen-month-old Amanda brings him several trains; everyone knows they are his favorite toy. He throws them over the gate. One teacher successfully redirects him to a puzzle.

Later, the other teacher picks up the trains and returns them to their bin. Amanda peers into the bins. She looks around the room, and when she sees Matthew, her face lights up. She brings the trains over and silently puts them on the table beside him. Seventeen-month-old Colin walks by the table, picks up the trains, and walks away. Matthew cries out and begins to chase Colin. Matthew moves to a corner, crying loudly, and throws several toys. He has a large bell in his hand as Amanda approaches with another train she has found; she offers it to him. He puts the bell down, takes the train, and sits on the carpet, holding it. Amanda returns to reading books with Emma and a student teacher. Matthew puts down the train, goes to a bookshelf, picks out a book, and joins them. He is much happier for the rest of the morning.

In this example, Amanda is persistent about helping Matthew. As Quann and Wein point out, Amanda's solution is more fine-tuned than the teacher's ideas.

- **Self-corrective empathy:** A child causes another child's distress and then tries to remedy it.

    Madison and Tony play quietly with puzzles on a rug. When Tony stands up, he accidentally bumps into Madison, who had started to stand, too. Tony reaches out and calmly pats Madison on the back.

Toddlers seem to understand that when others feel sad, they express it with tears, sad faces, and slumping bodies. They "feel with" other children.

The action part of empathy is to comfort others. We often see very young children engage in heartfelt attempts to comfort others. After observing two-year-olds, researcher Lois Murphy recorded examples of children comforting others, removing the cause of distress, or protecting other children, like the following one of little Heinrich:

Heinrich was on the kiddie car. Wallis was on the bicycle nearby. Wallis fell off the bicycle and pulled it over on himself. He wiggled and struggled to get out. Heinrich left the kiddie car and pulled the bike so that Wallis could get out. He rode off as soon as Wallis jumped up (Murphy, 1936).

Murphy found that two-year-olds will comfort other children with pats, hugs, kisses, and solicitous expressions such as, "That hurts, doesn't it?" They will attempt to remove the cause of another's distress. They will help a child out of physical distress by, for example, picking a child up after a fall. They will protect another child from harm, such as by catching a child as he falls or warning a child by saying, "You might fall." They suggest solutions, such as telling an adult to keep a child out of danger.

Two-year-olds whom Murphy observed had a repertoire of sympathetic behaviors that comforted, helped, and protected other children; warned other children about danger; and even suggested solutions to adults about how to help others. These young children responded to physical dilemmas such as accidents, falls, and needing bandages.

How do toddlers develop empathy? Toddlers do seem to be able to think of the other, but some children demonstrate more empathy than others. Several factors may contribute to a child's empathetic abilities. Young children generally need to know the difference between self and others, or *theory of mind*, to show empathy toward another person and attempt to alleviate the other person's distress. Young children demonstrate this capacity much earlier than previously thought (Kawakami et al., 2015). In addition, toddlers who know and use more emotion words (*sad, happy, frustrated*) are more empathic to their peers (Nichols et al., 2009). Affection between two toddlers also increases their empathic responses. Children who like each other seem to understand each other's emotions and reactions (Howes and Farver, 1992). Last, adult sensitivity to children's needs plays a vital part. It is important to remember that when empathic caregiving is modeled, children's development of empathy is more likely to occur. Empathy must be demonstrated, encouraged, and felt by very young children before they can develop an empathic disposition (Nichols et al., 2009).

We know that older toddlers are just learning the meanings of *taking turns, sharing, possessing,* and *owning.* We often use the word *sharing* when we really mean *turn-taking. Sharing* means dividing a number of items, such as toys or food, among a group. Many eighteen-month-olds can share when asked, and most twenty-four-month-olds can share without being asked.

Researchers gave plates of O-shaped cereal to young toddlers between the ages of eighteen and twenty-four months. When an adult placed a plate of cereal in front of a toddler, but then sighed and looked toward the items, only 25 percent of the eighteen-month-olds shared without being asked. But, 75 percent of the twenty-four-month-olds did share without being asked. When the adult held out his hand or verbally requested some cereal, 50 percent of the eighteen-month-olds and almost all the twenty-four-month-olds shared (Brownell et al., 2013). Young children often need adult cues to remember to share.

In another study, however, eighteen- to twenty-four-month-olds willingly shared toys such as marbles with each other. These results suggest that young children are not selfish but are generous with resources when they are dividing them among themselves (Ulber et al., 2015).

> "They [peers] are more likely to initiate play, direct positive affect to, and engage in complex interactions with familiar than with unfamiliar playmates" (Howes, 1988, cited in Shonkoff and Phillips, 2000).

Jed and Beth are sitting in cube chairs, with upside-down cube chairs in front of each of them serving as tables. Each child has a cup from dramatic play. Beth looks in her cup and puts in some O-shaped cereal from a bag she has brought from home. Beth looks at Jed and asks, "Do you have some?" Jed looks in his cup and shakes his head no. Beth reaches into her bag and fills his cup. They continue to eat (Whaley and Rubenstein, 1994).

Toddlers can make a friend, be a friend, and have a friend. In her study of toddlers in a child-care setting, Carolee Howes (2000) found that over half of the children had friendships that lasted over the year they were studied and that the friendships appeared sometime after children's first birthdays.

At fifteen months of age, a child was very excited to see his friend after being separated for four months. They squealed with recognition, tentatively touched each other, and then hugged and kissed each other (Howes, 2000).

Toddlers will look to the door to see if their friend has arrived for the day. They enjoy being with a friend and may hug, kiss, and play in a special way with their friend. Toddler friends help each other, share, and play more complex games than they do with other peers. In friendship, children have a genuine affection for each other. They want to spend more time with each other, and they even miss each other when apart. Toddlers do not have one set of behaviors that they use consistently with all children. They can develop friendships with certain children while not being friends with others.

Two girls were observed for an extended period in their infant-toddler group in an early care and learning center. Emily was fourteen months old; Katie was thirteen months old. They were affectionate with each other and showed they cared for each other by touching or trying to wipe the other's nose. They had a playful relationship—imitating each other, initiating games, gesturing, and vocalizing with each other. The two children, whom the teachers described as friends, preferred each other and engaged in reciprocal play (Shin, 2010).

Kimberly Whaley and Tamara Rubenstein (1994) observed in over two hundred hours of video how a group of toddler friends, ages twenty-two to thirty-six months, interacted with each other. In their article "How Toddlers 'Do' Friendship," the researchers considered children to be friends when the toddlers:

- had opportunities in their daily lives for regular play interactions with a specific partner;
- the partners were sufficiently well acquainted to have constructed scripted social interactions;
- companionship, intimacy, and affection could be inferred from these interactions; and
- the children preferred to be with each other.

Whaley and Rubenstein identified six dimensions that were present in the two-year-olds' friendships they observed: helping, intimacy, loyalty, sharing, similarity, and ritual activity. Children showed their loyalty by supporting their friend in the presence of other children.

Beth and Jed have been playing with the balls for about fifteen minutes when a teacher interrupts to take Jed for a diaper change. While he is in the bathroom, Harry walks across the room and picks up the red ball Jed has been using. Beth watches this and then turns and runs to the back of the room. She reaches into the basket holding the balls and gets a yellow ball out. Beth takes the yellow ball to Harry and reaches for the red one saying, "Jed's ball." Beth hands the yellow ball to Harry, who continues to play using this ball. Beth walks toward the bathroom with both her ball and Jed's in her arms (Whaley and Rubenstein, 1994).

Through mostly nonverbal means, Beth defended her own objects as well as her friend's. Young children in friendships may also imitate each other to create similarity and a "we're together" feeling.

Carly and Orly have been playing together, imitating one another for thirty-five minutes, when Orly begins running around the large table in the room singing "Ring around the Rosie" at the top of her lungs. Carly follows and runs behind Orly, singing along. Orly is wearing blue jeans that are slightly too big, and Carly has on a one-piece jumpsuit. While running, Orly's pants begin to fall down, so she reaches behind her and grabs her pants with her right hand to keep them up while running. Almost immediately, Carly reaches back with her right hand, grabs the back of her jumpsuit in the same place and continues to run with Orly (Whaley and Rubenstein, 1994).

These experiences give two-year-olds a sense of emotional and physical connection to each other. Prior to using language, nonverbal imitation binds two children together. The feature of imitation that distinguishes imitation between friends from imitation with other children who are not friends is its exactness. Between friends, imitation leads to a synchrony. Even when this synchrony was disrupted by a teacher, the two-year-olds return to imitations so closely matched that it is often difficult to determine which child is leading the interaction (Whaley and Rubenstein, 1994).

Games such as playing babies, bears, and monsters are just a few rituals observed among toddler friends. Toddlers in a different program developed specific games with their friends, played them only with their friends, and seemed to look forward to playing them.

Friends Zack and Maria are two years old. They have been together in the same class since they were infants. They spend a great deal of time together when they are in their school. Zack and Maria prefer to be together, selecting each other as partners over others in the group. These two children gain pleasure in being together and have favorite games they play with each other. They tell each other, "I love you." Because they have been together in the program since they were infants, they have had time together and continuity of group.

Not only do young children make friends, but toddlers grieve when relationships end (Whaley and Rubenstein, 1994). A toddler teacher at Boulder Journey School in Colorado captured how a child in her room seemed to remember and grieve for her friend who had to move to another room in the school.

Charley, a toddler girl, looks at an *All about Me* book of a classmate, Olivia, whose mother had to change the days that her child attended the school. An *All about Me* book has pictures of a child beginning when that child is a baby. Maria finds Olivia's book almost every day and looks through it. We do not positively know if she is grieving about not seeing Olivia in her room every day, but she does seem to have Olivia in mind.

> "A day without a friend is like a pot without a single drop of honey left inside."
>
> —Winnie the Pooh

Familiarity and friendship among toddlers is an important part of their lives. Friendships are fun. They allow children to practice relationship skills more deeply, and they foster empathy. Toddlers are three times more likely to respond to a friend in distress than to another playmate who is not their friend (Howes and Farver, 1987).

Do young children change their behavior in response to other children's behavior? Toddlers in the following example could change their language when playing with Sammy.

Sammy has cerebral palsy and can make clucking noises with his tongue. Without a teacher telling them to, two toddlers go to where he is lying on a couch. They begin to make clucking noises to him, while standing beside the couch looking over him at his face. He makes the noises, they imitate it, and Sammy breaks out in laughter. They are accommodating their language to the sounds that he can make. Rather than using language that Sammy could not use to communicate, they accommodate their language to his. They speak his language.

When toddlers adapt their behavior to another child's skill level, they are demonstrating social competence.

When infants and toddlers laugh, show delight, and experience joy and hilarity with each other, they are demonstrating toddler glee (Løkken, 2000a, 2000b). With glee, toddlers feel safe with each other and give of themselves in an emotional connection that brings a smile to their mouths and laughter to their bellies. Toddler glee may take many forms, such as dancing or running together, shrieking, laughing, or making noises together, rolling down a hill together, or even playing a "hilarious" game of spitting on one another. When we truly laugh with another adult, we abandon caution and feel almost as one with that person. We are in harmony with each other. We find the same things funny. We cement our relationships through laughter. When toddlers laugh with each other, their relationships become stronger as well. With joy as the goal, more toddler glee will erupt in programs for young children.

> "With children, it is the joint moments of delight that build the social brain."
>
> —Mariah Moser, somatic psychotherapist

Table 5: Prosocial Development and Learning Chart (Birth to 3)

Age	Prosocial Behavior
4–8 months	• Infants coo, smile, and laugh at each other (Porter, 2003). • Most five- and ten-month-olds make social judgments by choosing a helper puppet over one that is antisocial (Hamlin and Wynn, 2011). • Six- and ten-month-old infants assess individuals based on their behavior toward others. Infants prefer an individual who helps another to one who hinders another, prefer a helping individual to a neutral individual, and prefer a neutral individual to a hindering individual (Hamlin, Wynn, and Bloom, 2007).
8–12 months	• There is evidence of baby empathy—empathic concern and prosocial behavior in the first year of life for peers (Liddle, Bradley, and Mcgrath, 2015). • Some children eight and ten months of age show concern for their mothers who are exhibiting distress. These children vocalize, gesture, or show concerned facial expressions (Roth-Hanania et al., 2011). • Children from eight to twelve months old try to comfort other babies in distress. They smile, make sounds, wave, kick and swing their legs, and shake their heads side to side toward an infant who is crying (Liddle, Bradley, and Mcgrath, 2015). • Older infants show affection to adults and peers (McMullen et al., 2009). • Nine-month-olds look to adults to help other infants (Köster, Ohmer, Nguyen, and Kärtner, 2016).
12–18 months	• Prosocial behavior is present. Toddlers retrieve an out-of-reach object accidentally dropped by an adult experimenter (Warneken and Thomasello, 2007). • Children twelve to eighteen months old give their toys to parents after the parent prompts or after being reinforced by praise (Parke et al., 2010). • Children twelve and eighteen months old spontaneously will warn an adult by pointing out to her a hidden aversive object. Results show that infants intervene spontaneously to help others avoid a problem before it has occurred (Knudsen and Liszkowski, 2013). • Sixteen-month-olds choose to eat what prosocial puppets eat rather than what unfriendly puppets eat (Hamlin, and Wynn, 2012). • Preferences for another child can begin around twelve months (Howes, 2000). • Toddler friends exhibit strong preferences for each other and share caring, affective, playful, and humorous relationships (Shin, 2010). • Toddler friendship is proximity seeking, wanting to be close and to show affection such as smiling, laughing and hugging (Whaley and Rubenstein, 1994).

Age	Prosocial Behavior
18–24 months	• Toddlers prefer prosocial characters in a cartoon, indicating their preference for prosociality (Scola, Holvoet, Arciszewski, and Picard, 2015). • Children from eighteen to thirty months of age help peers that need help (Hepach, Kante, and Tomasello, 2016). • Toddlers demonstrate three types of empathy—proximal, altruistic, and self-corrective (Quann and Wein, 2006). • Eighteen-month-old children help adults whether the adult recipient is present or not (Hepach, Haberi, Lambert, and Tomasello, 2017). • Most toddlers can show kindness to others who are feeling distressed. Toddlers, however, may assume that what will comfort them will also comfort the distressed child. So, the one child may offer his blanket or bottle to the hurt or sad child (Zahn-Waxler, Radke-Yarrow, and King, 1979). • Some toddlers are capable of offering help to others who are hurt or sad. Some may have an impressive repertoire of altruistic behavior, and if one thing doesn't work they will try another way (Zahn-Waxler, Radke-Yarrow, and King, 1979). • Between eighteen and twenty-four months of age, other-oriented resource sharing becomes more frequent, spontaneous, and autonomous, with less need for support and encouragement from the recipient (Brownell, Lesue, Nichols, and Svetlova, 2013). • Children from eighteen to twenty-four months of age divide resources equally. These results suggest that young children are generous with resources when they are dividing them among themselves (Ulber, Hamann, and Tomasello, 2015). • Friends are more likely to touch, lean on, and smile at each other than are children who are not friends. • Friends prefer each other as interaction partners (Whaley and Rubenstein, 1994).

24–36 months	• Older toddlers can behave prosocially:
	
	  » comforting other children with pats, hugs, and kisses
	
	  » attempting to remove the cause of another's distress
	
	  » protecting another child
	
	  » warning another child
	
	  » suggesting solutions to peer problems (Murphy, 1936)
	
	• By the age of two years, children voluntarily share valued resources with unrelated individuals when there is no cost to them for doing so. Notably, however, this depends on the recipient making her desire explicit (Brownell, Svetlove, and Nichols, 2009).
	
	• Older toddlers are intrinsically motivated to help others (Hepach, Vaish, and Tomasello, 2012). They are not motivated by extrinsic rewards. Praise that comments on the child's intrinsic motivation, however, is likely to facilitate prosocial behavior (Warneken and Tomasello, 2008).

Age	Prosocial Behavior
24–36 months (cont'd.)	• Older toddlers begin to understand fairness (Geraci and Surian, 2011).
	• Older toddlers are prosocial even when their adult partners are not (Sebastián-Enesco, Hernández-Lloreda, and Colmenares, 2013).
	• Two-year-olds are caregivers, not just care receivers (Kawakami and Takai-Kawakami, 2015).
	• Two-year-olds nurture infants in gentle, respectful ways in a multiage classroom (McGaha, Cummings, Lippard, and Dallas, 2011).
	• Six dimensions are present in two-year-olds' friendships: helping, intimacy, loyalty, sharing, similarity, and ritual activity (Whaley and Rubenstein, 1994).
	• Children can express glee—they laugh, show delight, and experience joy and hilarity with each other (Løkken, 2000a, 2000b).
	• Two- to three-year-olds who are part of a training group to teach them about emotions display gains in emotion understanding (Grazzani, Ornaghi, Agliati, and Brazzelli, 2016).
	• There is a strong relationship between emotion understanding at the age of three and prosocial behavior at the age of four (Ensor, Spencer, and Hughes, 2011).

Individual and Group Differences

Temperament, gender, and culture play a part in how young children interact with peers in prosocial ways.

Temperament

Young children who are inhibited, reserved, or withdrawn need kind support to venture out with peers while holding a teacher's or a parent's hand. With gradual and patient help, these children become more familiar with the adults and children in their lives (Fox et al., 2013). Some newborns and infants seem irritable. Adults will need to figure out how to touch and hold them in ways that comfort them. If newborns who are irritable experience responsive, secure attachments, they are more likely to explore and be sociable as toddlers (Stupica, 2011).

Children who are considered emotionally negative may frown a great deal, whine frequently, feel fearful, and be quick to anger (Spinrad and Stifter, 2006).

These children have a difficult time playing happily with peers. They must have responsive adults in their lives who understand this type of temperament and are not critical, but instead are warm, open, and emotionally available (Kim and Kochanska, 2012). Comfort these children when they are distressed, and go with them to be with their peers after they feel very safe with you.

Provide support for children who are exuberant and have difficulty regulating their exuberance. They are often in the middle of the action and may need help hugging gently, talking softly, and being careful not to bump other children as they jump around. Help children who hurt others and who are rejected by others.

Gender

You may have heard that girls are more prosocial than boys. However, a study by Ronit Roth-Hanania, Maayan Davidov, and Carolyn Zahn-Waxler showed no differences between eight- to sixteen-month-old boys' and girls' prosocial responses to their mother's distress (Roth-Hanania, Davidov, and Zahn-Waxler, 2011). Research found no gender differences in how twenty-four-month-old children responded with concern when they heard a crying infant (Nichols, Svetlova, and Brownell, 2015). Studies of preschool children, however, have found that girls are more empathic than boys (according to the children's teachers) (Belacchi and Farina, 2012). Teachers will want to promote prosocial behavior in both boys and girls to counteract the gender differences or stereotypes that may have influence by the preschool years.

Culture

Cultural values influence toddlers' prosocial behavior. According to Moritz Köster and his colleagues from Germany and Brazil, mothers in Brazil support their toddlers' helping behavior by *assertive scaffolding*—serious and insistent requesting. Mothers in Germany are more likely to use deliberate scaffolding to encourage their children to help in tasks. *Deliberate scaffolding* includes asking, pleading, and giving insistent requests. Children in Brazil are more likely to help if they hear assertive scaffolding, while children in Germany are more likely to help if they hear deliberate scaffolding.

This research is important for educators. The results tell us that there are culture-specific ways that children are socialized to help (Köster et al., 2016). Teachers who politely ask children to help (deliberate scaffolding) may wonder why the children do not respond. Teachers may think that the children are being deliberately disobedient. Instead, the children may have learned prosocial behavior within a culture and are unfamiliar with other adult styles of requesting that the child help. Teachers will need to investigate any cultural differences, patiently respect these differences, interview families for their viewpoints and practices, and gently help children learn that there are various ways an adult may request prosocial behavior.

Infants and toddlers have a caring capacity. They are capable of being and becoming prosocial—being kind, feeling empathy, and comforting others. When young children are prosocial they help and comfort their peers. They show warmth and affection, share space and toys, cooperate with each other, and show empathy, compassion, and understanding of others.

Infants figure out who is nice, show affect, expect adults to help others, and develop and communicate beginning empathy for others. Toddlers grow in their ability to help, feel empathy, comfort others, share, develop friendships, and share glee. Temperament, gender, and culture influence children's prosocial development and behavior.

In the next chapter, we will look at ways that caregivers can support infants and toddlers in developing their caring capacities.

Chapter FIVE

Strategies for Supporting Development
of the Caring Capacities

Strategies That Make a Difference

Children ages birth to three need your guidance to become prosocial (Gross et al., 2015). Children generally have a natural tendency to help others; however, this tendency must be nurtured by their culture, families, teachers, and by all the adults in their lives.

Think of yourself as offering *guided participation* (Rogoff et al., 2003). Guided participation includes setting up opportunities for children to be prosocial, sharing the activity with them, and adapting possibilities to the children's stage of development (Dahl, 2015). Children must experience what it is like to be prosocial with you, other adults, and peers. Helping children become prosocial requires adults to be prosocial detectors and opportunity providers.

> "The central idea is that infants have specific social experiences, involving requests, participation, and praising, that contribute to the emergence and development of helping" (Dahl, 2015).

Reflect, Observe, and Document

Prosocial behaviors may be occurring more than a teacher might think. Aggressive or hurtful behaviors often cause a distraction in the home or center; make a point to look for the prosocial behaviors that are happening as well. Adults will want to attend with enthusiasm, affirmation, and encouragement to support young children in showing empathy, comforting, and helping others.

Observing and documenting children's prosocial attempts, attitudes, and behavior makes the wonderful caring capacities of infants and toddlers visible to the children, teachers, families, and the community. Capturing children's kind behaviors motivates teachers to think about ways to encourage even more thoughtful behaviors among children. Capture prosocial moments with photos or video. Create display boards and look at them and at videos with the young children. As you watch videos together, ask the children questions about what you are seeing. For example, ask a small group of older toddlers, "What did Ade do to help Athena (who was crying)?" or "What would you do to help Athena?" This both acknowledges prosocial behavior and encourages social problem solving.

Ask the following questions as you observe young children's prosocial behavior.

With infants:

- When do infants smile and/or laugh at each other?
- How do infants respond to adults' and peers' angry or fearful faces?
- How do infants react to another infant in distress? Do you see attempts to comfort distressed infant peers?
- How do infants show affection to each other?
- How can you tell if infants are enjoying each other?

With toddlers:

- How do children help each other?
- How do children demonstrate friendship?
- How do children initiate interactions with their peers?
- How do children comfort and/or show kindness to each other?
- What types of empathy do you see—proximal, altruistic, and/or self-corrective?

- How do children demonstrate prosocial behavior—comfort, attempt to remove the cause of another's distress, protect another child, warn another child, suggest solutions to a peer's problem?

- What are the cultural differences related to learning prosocial behaviors that children experience in their families?

Observing helps us understand the intentions of children. In an article on promoting prosocial behavior in infants and toddlers, Linda Gillespie and Amy Hunter (2010) share a wonderful example of how understanding children's development and observing their behavior resulted in toddlers' sharing a prosocial experience.

Children in a toddler room were playing with their five plastic bangle bracelets that the teacher had given each of them. Josh put all his bracelets on his arm and then looked around for more. He reached over and took Sasha's bracelets and started putting them on his arm. Of course, Sasha protested and said, "Mine."

Josh's teacher observed that Josh's goal was to put all the bracelets on his arm. She said, "Sasha, let's watch Josh and see what he is going to do. Josh is trying to fill up his whole arm with bracelets." Sasha looked and then gave Josh one of her bracelets. Other toddlers began sharing their bracelets with Josh, too. "Wow!" the teacher said, "Look what you all did. Josh's whole arm is filled with the bracelets!" The teacher took a photo to document how pleased all the children were with how they helped Josh.

At other times, teachers will help Josh ask before he takes the toys of other children; however, in this moment the teacher helped the toddlers take the perspective of a peer. Instead of assuming negative intentions, the children learned to think of others' intentions and goals.

Use Adult-Child Relationship-Based Strategies

Experiences in early relationships make a difference in prosocial behavior (Newton et al., 2016). Children become prosocial in their first relationships and the activities that they share with them (Brownell, 2013). Adults who develop relationships with infants and toddlers use a variety of strategies to help them learn to comfort others, think about others' perspectives, and feel empathy for others.

In this book, we emphasize how important modeling and sensitivity of adults to young children are for their prosocial dispositions (Newton et al., 2016). Sensitivity starts with figuring out what children are feeling and thinking. It then involves kindness, compassion, and warmth toward children. Relationship-based strategies include using mind-mindedness, assuming good intentions, and encouraging and supporting peer interactions.

Use Mind-Mindedness Strategies

Using mind-mindedness strategies with children supports their prosocial behavior (Newton et al., 2016). Mind-mindedness (as well as sensitivity) involves adults trying to understand the child's perspective, including why she might be behaving in a certain way. It involves talking with the child about her feelings, wishes, and intentions. When an adult says, "It seems you are feeling angry. It was hard for you when you couldn't put on your shoe," the adult is "reading" the mind of the child. This requires familiarity with the child, her habits, and her temperament. When teachers use mind-mindedness strategies, they build strong emotional bonds with the children.

Keep in mind the four *E*s: emphasize, embrace, encourage, and enable prosocial behaviors to affirm children. When adults practice these four approaches, children are more likely to be prosocial (Gross et al., 2015). Use specific affirmations to encourage infants' and toddlers' prosocial pats, hugs, helping, and guiding others: "Rosa, you helped Damont find his shoes. He really liked that. You are a great helper." With affirmation, young children not only realize they get attention for these behaviors, but they also will develop an identity of themselves as people who are prosocial.

Conscientiously create a prosocial feeling and emphasize these attitudes in your care setting. When prosocial behavior is valued, the children sense and learn the importance of kind-heartedness.

Teachers often wonder whether they should reward children's prosocial behavior. Several researchers who have studied children's natural altruistic tendencies have found that extrinsic rewards interfere with children's prosocial behavior. Children begin to concentrate on the reward rather than on the prosocial behavior. Commenting and encouraging, however, are likely to increase prosocial behavior because adults are emphasizing the child's own kindness, pointing out the prosocial effects on other children and focusing on the child's effort (Warneken and Tomasello, 2008).

Use Emotion Talk and Coaching

> Abdalla, a two-and-a-half-year-old, ran to his friend who was crying and said, "You feel sad? Me feel sad." Abdalla was expressing *emotion understanding* (EU), the ability to recognize and understand one's own and others' emotions.

EU is directly related to children's social competence. When children understand their own and their peers' emotions, they are more likely to be prosocial with them (Ensor et al., 2011).

In a study by Ilaria Grazzani and colleagues, teachers of two- to three-year-old children were taught how to support toddlers' EU. Teachers in the experimental group met with a small group of children for a short period four times a week. Each teacher read an illustrated story and then talked with

the children about the emotions featured in the story. For example, in a story about two rabbits, the rabbits at times feel scared, happy, angry, mad, or sad. The teacher then talked with the children about what makes them feel angry, scared, happy, mad, or sad, focusing on one feeling each time. The teacher asked questions such as, "Is there anything else that makes you angry?" "What kind of face do you make when you are angry?" The toddlers who heard the stories and engaged in conversations about them improved in EU and prosocial behavior compared to a group who didn't hear stories (Grazzani et al., 2016).

Use emotion talk and coach children to learn and use emotion words. In research by Michelle Lauw and colleagues, parents of toddlers were taught to not dismiss their children's emotions in an emotion-coaching parenting program called "Tuning in to Kids." Parents acknowledged their children's emotions and talked about them with their children. Over six months, as parents coached their children to use emotion talk, the toddlers' acting-out behavior improved (Lauw et al., 2014).

Meet individual children's emotional needs by responding to their cries, comforting them when they are distressed, and using emotion words. They then will be more likely to show empathy for their peers' distress. To become prosocial with others, infants and toddlers need to feel what it is like to be treated prosocially and need to learn emotion understanding.

Model, Model, and Model Some More

One of the most powerful strategies that adults use to encourage prosocial behavior is to model it continuously. Show children how to be kind and how to help others. They are learning from adults how to be with others. Model appreciation, thanking a child who holds up one arm to help you put on her shirt (Honig, 2014). When you see a child in need, take another infant or toddler with you to see what is wrong and provide comfort. Model how to be caring, helpful, and comforting to others. In a study by Rebecca Williamson, Meghan Donohue, and Erin Tully, two-year-olds watched a short video of an adult performing a novel prosocial behavior in response to another person's distress. The two-year-olds then had a chance to imitate the novel behavior with their own parent who was in physical distress. The children who saw the short video were more prosocial toward their parents, using both the novel prosocial behavior and other prosocial behaviors that weren't modeled, such as hugging, kissing, and verbally comforting, that weren't modeled. The children who watched the video seemed to want to alleviate the parent's pain more than the other groups who didn't see the video (Williamson et al., 2012). Young children are constantly learning through observing others.

What to Do about Sharing

Do you encourage children to share, or not? Sharing is one of the most difficult challenges for teachers of young children. One-year-olds and young toddlers will not understand if you tell them to share. Older toddlers, however, can begin learning the concepts of sharing, taking turns, possession, and ownership. If, for example, a child has a toy, puts it down, walks away, and then wants it back from the child who picked it up, say, "Kareem has the toy now. When he is finished, then you can have it." If a child brings a toy from home, you may say, "Everett owns the toy. Ask him if you can play with it." If a child has a toy that another child wants, then encourage the first child to say, "Can I have a turn?" You can use the word *share* when passing food around the table: "We are sharing our food today. Matias has some, and Anna has some. We are sharing." Or, "Stephen had two trucks and he gave one to Alex. He shared his toy."

There are many times when you wouldn't expect a child to share. If a child is focusing on completing a task with several trucks, then support that child's persistence and self-regulation. You can encourage the second child to ask if she can play with the toys after the first child is done with them. Often, you will have to offer the words for young children to use in these situations or offer alternative toys or activities. When children must wait, they will need help from adults to understand and find something else to do.

Support Children's Communication with Each Other

Teaching infants and toddlers to use sign language for *stop, help*, and *more* can help children feel more self-control during peer interactions. Model descriptive language and encourage children to use the words as they interact with their peers.

Emphasize Perspective Taking and Problem Solving

Understanding another's point of view is difficult for adults, but we can listen to another's words and watch physical cues to determine how others feel. Young children are just learning about their own and other's feelings and need constant support to think about a peer's emotional state or the intentions of another. Help toddlers notice another child in distress and think about how to help the other child who is feeling blue, crying, or having difficulty with a task. For example, say to a child, "I think Shawn is feeling sad. Look. He is crying. What could we do to help him feel better?" If the child has difficulty thinking of a helpful solution, then offer two choices and let the helping toddler decide. Or, support the helping toddler to offer two choices to the child who is sad.

> "Shame is considered an inhibitor of prosocial behavior; whereas, guilt is considered a motivator" (Drummond et al., 2016).

Rather than shaming children, help them fix the problem. Shaming children includes embarrassing them, telling them they should be ashamed, and humiliating them. Shaming is demeaning, belittling, and condescending. Help children make reparations, if for example, they have broken another child's toy. Problem solve how to fix the toy or help the children figure out how to help the ones they hurt.

Jesse Drummond and colleagues (2016) observed that toddlers, average age twenty-nine months, responded naturally with either a shamelike or a guiltlike response when they were led to believe that they had broken an adult's toy. Shamelike responses included avoiding the adult and seldom confessing or attempting to repair the toy. Guiltlike responses included confessing their behavior and attempting to repair the toy. The toddlers who showed guiltlike responses to the broken toy were later more likely to help an adult in emotional distress faster and more frequently. Shame seemed to cause the children to avoid the one they hurt, possibly in fear of being shamed again. They focused on themselves rather than on the other. Shaming children does not help them become prosocial.

Create a Caring Community—Environments and Responsive Program Planning

The environments and programs we create for children demonstrate and reveal our respect for their active learning capabilities, their sociability, and their individuality. Carefully and thoughtfully crafted environments and program organizations give clear messages that we care for young children and deem them worthy of the most interesting, responsive, socially supportive, and motivating atmospheres we can create.

Environments

Prosocial environments support children's experience of each other as kind, helpful, loyal, and empathic. Teachers can arrange the physical environment with cozy corners for two and can provide play centers for two or three children. Duplicate toys encourage imitation and children's sense of similarity to others.

Teachers can thoughtfully plan for relationships to happen each day. As adults observe the interests and goals of each individual child, they can change the environment, add materials, or create other opportunities for children to build relationships with peers and adults. Children can choose from interesting and well-displayed opportunities for exploration, while supportive adults are available for the children to refuel emotionally when they need to. As children choose, they naturally interact with each other.

> "The environment should act as an aquarium that reflects the ideas, ethics, attitudes, and culture of the people who live in it. This is what we are working toward."
>
> —Loris Malaguzzi, founder of the Reggio Emilia approach

Continuity of Care and Groups in Programs

Because friendships are more likely to occur after children have spent time together, teachers need to reconsider any policy that moves children to another classroom every six to twelve months or that separates a child from her group when she has a birthday or when she reaches a motor milestone such as walking. Keeping a group together supports familiarity, friendship, and prosocial behavior. Peers who are familiar with each other are more likely to initiate play, be more positive, and engage in more complex interactions (Howes, 1988). Besides, it is a scary, lonely experience for a child to move to another room without the familiar faces of teachers and peers. One toddler did not want to turn three years old because she knew she would move alone from the toddler to the preschool room. It seems very sad that a two-year-old would not look forward to her birthday. Entering a new group is challenging for adults—imagine what it is like for young children.

Support Families

Parents want to know what to focus on in the early years with their children to help encourage healthy social development. We've learned much from interviewing and observing parents and from research.

We know that parents' sensitivity—warmth, kindness, and ability to read cues such as hunger—and their empathetic behavior with their children results in children who are more prosocial (Blandon and Scrimgeour, 2015). Parents of children who are prosocial are not permissive about their children hurting others (Christopher et al., 2013; Dahl, 2016); instead, they give intense messages that their children must not hurt others. For example, a parent might firmly say to her child who has kicked another child, "No kicking. Kicking hurts. Look—your friend is crying."

Parents of prosocial children try very hard to never spank or hit their children, because they know that if they do they are modeling inappropriate behavior. They've learned that spanking doesn't teach children what prosocial behaviors to use. Rather, parents of prosocial children help their children see the connection between what they do and how it affects another child. For instance, "You bit her. That hurt her." They give reasons and explanations for why the child should or should not behave in a specific way. They do not just say *no* or *stop*. They use emotionally expressive language. They teach their children what to do instead of biting or hitting. A parent might say, "Pat gently—it feels good when you pat gently." They are kind and loving toward their children. They give hugs and kisses. The parents model for their children how to help others. As a result, the children imitate their parents, expect kindness from others, and use the same prosocial behaviors with their peers (Zahn-Waxler et al., 1992).

Summary of Strategies

- Reflect, observe, and document:

  » Reflect on your role, offering guided participation to children throughout the early years to support their prosocial learning.

  » Reflect on your role as a prosocial detector and equal-opportunity provider. Create a prosocial ambiance in your program.

  » Observe and document the often subtle but clearly visible prosocial attitudes and behaviors of infants and toddlers.

  » Capture prosocial moments with photos and videos. Look at these with the children. Encourage the children to talk about what they do to be helpful and kind to peers.

  » Create documentation panels that explain what happened between peers, the prosocial strategies used, and the outcomes. Share the documentation with families, too.

- Use adult-child relationship-based strategies:

  » Help children feel relationship competent. How you are with young children makes a difference in how they are with peers.

  » Use the four *E*s strategy: emphasize, embrace, encourage, and enable prosocial behavior.

  » Affirm children's prosocial attitudes and behavior. With affirmation, young children will develop an identity as someone who is prosocial.

  » Use emotion talk and coaching to develop children's emotion understanding. Higher EU relates to more prosocial behavior.

  » Model, model, and model some more. Children learn through observing others.

  » Understand how difficult it is for children to share. They are learning the differences among the concepts of sharing, owning, possessing, and turn-taking.

  » Support children's communication with each other.

  » Help toddlers problem solve how to help other children.

  » Emphasize children's perspective taking and empathy for their peers.

  » Do not shame children when they hurt objects or others. Shame contributes to children focusing on themselves. Rather, help them focus on how to help the ones who are hurt or how to fix objects that are broken.

- Create a caring community:

  » Create a prosocial environment—cozy corners, interesting explorations, and duplicate toys.

  » Be available for children's emotional refueling.

  » Provide continuity of care and groups in programs.

- Support families:

  » Provide and discuss information for families on parental sensitivity and empathetic behavior. Help parents understand that these behaviors will result in children who are more prosocial.

  » Encourage and support parents in giving intense (nonpunitive) messages that their children must not hurt anyone.

  » Encourage and support parents in giving reasons for why children should behave prosocially and not hurt anyone.

  » Encourage and support parents in modeling kindness and helping.

Being prosocial involves children thinking of the other. Infant and toddler prosocial behavior includes helping, comforting, warning of danger, and showing empathy for adults and peers. Parents and professionals can support prosocial development by providing loving care and modeling kindness. They can support children's caring capacities, discuss feelings, encourage children's emotional self-regulation, support language development, and focus on reparations rather than shaming. They create environments of cozy corners, spaces for one or two, spaces for movement, and places for toddler rituals and routines. Children's prosocial abilities are further expanded when they are in a group of children with whom they are familiar, with which they move together as a group to the next room in a program, or with whom they stay while materials change to accommodate their growing interests. Teachers and parents can value the importance of friends in toddlers' lives and can support these friendships. Adults can provide opportunities for toddler glee that echoes across a room or outdoors, thoughtfully planning for prosocial relationships and ambiance in the program each day.

Chapter SIX

Peer Conflicts—Struggles and Learning

Fourteen-month-old Jeremy watches fifteen-month-old Deseree closely and then quickly moves in to take the toy that is in front of her. Deseree, who was just about to pick up the toy, begins to scream and grabs the toy back. The struggle continues with an all-out tug-of-war until the teacher moves in to help.

Where there are young children, there will be social conflict. Although we also know that children of this age can be quite prosocial, the type of conflict described in this example may occur often when very young children are together. Conflict happens when one or more children resist another child's actions, protest what another child is doing or saying, or retaliate for a perceived wrong. Conflicts among infants and toddlers are not usually aggressive, but they do involve complex emotions of anger, sadness, disappointment, and frustration. With the right kind of support from caring and responsive adults, conflicts are opportunities to help young children learn emotional, social, language, and cognitive dispositions and skills.

As we've discussed earlier, children from birth to three move toward social competence with responsive, caring adults who help them with self-regulation, social decisions, and prosocial behaviors. These very young children are learning how to use language, and they often solve problems physically. They are learning about power, dominance, and how to cooperate and negotiate with peers in play. It is no wonder that there are conflicts!

Conflicts, however, are prime occasions to build relationships among children and teachers. Conflicts can help children learn about themselves and others' needs. They are opportune times for toddlers to learn important problem-solving skills that will help them become socially competent.

From Biting to Hugging: Understanding Social Development in Infants and Toddlers

The Value of Conflict

Mari was ready to ask her director if she could move from teaching in the toddler room to teaching in the preschool room. It seemed as if all day long children were snatching toys from each other and making each other cry. She didn't know if she could take one more day. In desperation, she asked her director and coteachers if they could have a meeting to talk about the aggravating conflicts.

During the meeting, Mari learned that with toddlers conflicts are inevitable and have a great deal of value. She hadn't thought about how conflicts provided a wonderful opportunity to help young children learn. She realized now how important she and the teaching assistants were in the lives of these very young children. She and her team felt energized and ready to try some new strategies.

Conflicts are important teaching times for young children. Conflict differs from mean-spirited aggression and is a primary way young children learn about self and other, about feelings and empathy, cognitive and communications skills, and about how to become socially competent (Wittmer and Petersen, 2017). With the guidance of adults, conflicts help children attain social competence—the attitude and skills to enjoy being with others and to interact successfully with them to each person's satisfaction.

In young children, it is possible for social competence and conflict to have a positive, cyclical relationship—particularly with the help of understanding and knowledgeable adults. Socially competent children tend to be full of confidence and often right in the middle of the play action. This results in more opportunities for conflict with peers, but these conflicts can teach valuable lessons in social development at these ages.

Children Learn about Self and Other

With adult help, young children can gain a sense of self during conflicts. They learn what they can do and how they affect others. Conflicts are also opportunities for children to learn about self and other—how they are the same and different from others. They learn that others may think, act, and feel in ways other than they do. This idea, *theory of mind*, develops over the first years of life. During conflict,

peers learn about individual peer differences. They learn what toys other children like, how other children react when a toy is taken from them, and what will comfort a peer. These are valuable lessons to learn about others.

Children in conflict learn to observe their peers and to predict peers' behavior. Consider this example.

Two toddlers, each approximately thirteen months old, were riding on rocking horses near each other. A third rocking horse sat empty. As Toddler 1 and Toddler 2 rocked, they watched each other carefully without smiling. Toddler 2 moved off her horse. She approached Toddler 1 and pushed her off balance on her horse. At first, Toddler 1 protested but soon slid completely off and went to the third horse, while keeping a close eye on Toddler 2. Rocking continued, but as soon as Toddler 2 moved off the preferred horse, Toddler 1 swiftly moved to her initial horse and mounted it. Toddler 2 went back to her initial horse as well. When Toddler 1 spied her blanket across the room, she dismounted from her horse but, not wanting to leave her horse, she dragged it across the room as she retrieved her blanket (Hall and Forman, nd).

Toddler 1 seemed to know that if she left her horse for a second, Toddler 2 would likely snatch it. It is as if Toddler 1 were reading the mind of Toddler 2. These very young toddlers were learning about self and other during this mild conflict over who would ride which rocking horse.

Children are most successful during conflicts if they use strategies that involve less power and more negotiation while also thinking of the other's perspective—not an easy task for toddlers during conflicts.

Children Learn about Emotions, Empathy, and Self-Regulation

Through conflict, young children learn to identify and express their feelings, recognize others' feelings, develop empathy for others, think about shared feelings, and manage feelings with their peers. This happens if teachers model emotion words such as *happy, unhappy, sad, angry, disappointed,* and *excited* with the children, both during conflicts and at many other times. As children gradually learn and begin to use emotion words, they are more likely to manage their strong feelings.

Teachers can begin by helping children understand their feelings. When a child has a sad face, the teacher can say, "You look sad," while making a face like the child and talking about what is making the child sad. In noticing and commenting on the emotions of other children, the teacher can help children start to understand that others have feelings,

too. This gradual process develops into adulthood, so we cannot expect young children to have mastered the task. However, if a teacher is holding an older infant and sees a toddler crying, the teacher can say to the infant, "Eva is crying. She is sad. Let's go help Eva." At other times, the teacher can point to his own smile and say, "I'm happy. I'm smiling. The sun is shining, and we can go outdoors." If teachers persistently mention feelings, they will give children the gift of learning to understand themselves and others.

Self-regulation is the ability to manage one's emotions and impulses and to respond appropriately to one's environment. This set of skills is critical for young children to be successful in all areas of development. Interactions with others let children practice and improve their ability to control their emotions in healthy ways. A toddler who feels like

From Biting to Hugging: Understanding Social Development in Infants and Toddlers

kicking another but doesn't, or a child who is able to calm himself and return to playing after being upset is demonstrating self-regulation skills.

When parents and teachers are emotionally available, children's ability to recognize and control their emotions grows. They learn to manage feelings of distress, anger, and frustration with adult help.

When infants and toddlers are comforted by caring adults when they are hungry, in pain, or afraid, they learn how to become calm again. Children learn strategies for self-regulation, when, for example, a teacher asks a distressed child, "Would a hug help you?" or "Would holding a teddy bear help?" or "Would you like to rest in the cozy corner with your friend for a while?"

Children Learn Cognitive and Communication Skills

With the help from a responsive adult, children learn how to problem solve during conflict—discover alternative solutions and make choices to solve a peer problem. They learn to communicate, negotiate, and even cooperate to accomplish a task.

"Conflicts can be considered significant situations of communication, social learning, and problem solving" (Singer and Hannikainen, 2002).

The teacher asked two-year-olds Peter and Damion to carry a bucket of water to the other side of the playground where the children had planted flowers. The teacher knew that one child could not carry the bucket by himself. She wanted to see if the children could figure out how to cooperate to accomplish the task. Peter and Damion looked at each other and then at the bucket. Peter tried to pick it up but couldn't lift it. Damion pushed Peter's hands away and tried to pick it up, but he couldn't lift it either. Peter said, "Mine." Damion yelled back, "Mine!" The boys looked at each other again. Peter grabbed the handle with one hand and gestured to Damion to do the same. The boys dragged the bucket across the playground, stopping to rest often, while sloshing water all over the ground. They had cooperated and figured out a solution. After watering the flowers with the little water left in the bucket, the boys ran to the teacher to tell her, "More water!"

Conflicts give children experience with thinking about how their viewpoint is the same as or different from another child. As they practice this, they learn the negotiation and self-regulation skills necessary to prevent conflicts from escalating and interfering with play. Again, thoughtful adult guidance is imperative to helping children learn this.

Children Learn How to be Social and Prosocial

Social competence requires all the skills we've discussed, as well as sharing, understanding and respecting ownership and possession, knowing how to help others, and knowing how to show and receive affection. Conflicts provide an avenue for young children to begin learning these social and prosocial skills.

Sharing is difficult for young children. However, it is important to first recognize the many ways that young children do share. Infants share space with another infant on a teacher's lap. Toddlers share a painting table with other children. Two-year-olds share food if they pass bowls family-style from child to child at a table. When we broaden our thinking about sharing, we can appreciate the many ways young children share every day.

Teachers can help children share toys without demanding that they do so. Assist a child in finding the words to ask another child to let him hold a toy or use it for a while. Help a child wait if another child says no to his request for a toy. Doing so is scaffolding the child's ability to ask, share, and wait for a turn.

One reason that sharing is difficult and conflicts occur is because toddlers are just learning about ownership and how the concept of ownership is different from possession. By two years of age, children can begin to understand ownership. They may talk about "my hat" or "daddy's car."

Young children are learning that possession means that the child has temporary control of an object or a person. The child does not own the object and usually cannot keep it forever. Toddlers are likely to think if they possess a toy that it is their toy until they do not want it anymore. They may think it is their toy, even though they walk away from it for a while. Toddlers may understand and say "mine" but still have a difficult time recognizing that taking someone's possession is unjust (Brownell et al., 2009).

Adults who want to reduce the number of conflicts will help children learn the vocabulary for *mine, yours,* possession, and ownership. The children will not only learn the meaning of the concepts, they also will share and take turns more frequently (Hay, 2006).

We know that children's involvement in conflict plays a positive role in peer development as they begin to learn that others have ideas that are different from their own. They learn to communicate and problem solve and learn how to express feelings and empathy. There is potential for children to progress or regress in social competence, depending on the child, the setting, and the adults who scaffold conflict resolution—or not.

Types of Conflict

Besides the fact that infants, young toddlers, and older toddlers are in the process of learning and practicing social skills, there are many other reasons for conflicts. When we understand why conflicts may occur, we can begin to reduce their numbers. When children do engage in conflicts, we can help them grow emotionally and socially.

Many conflicts arise from well-intentioned actions. Consider conflicts from the child's perspective by thinking about the child's goals. A grab for a toy from another may be an awkward (and often unsuccessful) attempt to play with the other child (Williams et al., 2007). A lunge toward another or knocking down a peer's block structure may be an attempt to get the other child's attention. A child who is just beginning to toddle may start to hug another toddler, only to bump into and fall on the other child. The knocked-down child understandably protests, and a conflict ensues. Once we know the many reasons for conflicts, however, we can begin to understand young children's goals. When we understand children's goals, we are taking their perspective and can begin to support their learning. The following lists the goals that infants and toddlers often have that can lead to conflict.

- **Exploration:** Children have a strong drive to explore. This is one of the ways that they learn. Their investigations may interrupt the activities of others. Peers may not want their noses or hair to be investigated by another child.

- **Interrupted activity and intrusion on personal space:** Young children often do not like to have interference when they are focused on a task. Older toddlers who are playing may not want other children to join them, or a child may resist a child who pushes him over.

- **Awakened needs:** Another child's activity may remind a child of a similar need and may lead to the child's taking or moving closer to a desired object or person.

- **Dominance:** Some children may use power techniques, such as yelling, telling, or forcing, to control other children.

- **Object use, possession, and ownership:** Toddlers are only beginning to understand the difference between possessing and owning an object. A child may start to play with a toy that another child possessed but abandoned. However, the first child may feel that, because he possessed the toy once, he has a right to it all day. A child may "own" an object and not want any other children to play with it.

- **Self-regulation challenges:** Young children are learning how to control their emotions, effort, attention, and behavior. Their brains are still developing, and they need support to learn how to express emotions in healthy ways and how to control their behavior.

Next, we look at the developmental reasons infants and toddlers experience conflict.

Conflict in Infants

Let's start with the reasons that infants may have conflict. Simple exploration, interrupted activity, and awakened needs are three primary reasons why infants experience conflict.

Simple Exploration

Researchers from Switzerland observed the same twenty-eight children when they were eight, fourteen, and twenty-two months old in a child-care setting (Licht, Simoni, and Perrig-Chiello, 2008). They found that conflicts occurred at all three ages because of the young children's need to explore. Another infant's or toddler's nose, a toy waving in another child's hand, or an interesting noise from another infant is of great interest to a curious young explorer. We know that infants and toddlers use all their senses to learn about the world; they must touch, taste, shake, and manipulate that nose, waving toy, or mouth of the child making a noise. This, of course, may cause the other child to protest loudly.

It is very important to remember that when an infant explores and reaches in to take a toy from another infant, the first infant's goal may be social. It may be as if the infant is saying, "You and the toy are interesting. I don't just want to play with the toy. I want to play with you!" Picture a crawling infant making his way across the blanket over to Justin, who is lying on his back not yet able to crawl. We can point out to the exploring child to be gentle and can demonstrate how to crawl around Justin. We can say to another child when he explores Manuel's nose, "Be gentle. That's Manuel's nose. See, you have a nose, too," while pointing to his nose.

Interrupted Activity

Ten-month-old Serena sits with a book, struggling to keep it on her lap. Francis, who walked at eleven months, sees the colorful book in Serena's hands. He watches Serena turn the colorful pages. Francis toddles over and lifts the book from Serena's lap. Serena's cries, causing Francis to drop the book and amble away. Serena picks up the book and continues looking at it.

It seems that continuing her activity is Serena's goal. We can admire older infants' perseverance at continuing a task. Infants are capable of being absorbed in an activity. No wonder they protest loudly when they are interrupted unexpectedly.

Awakened Needs

When one infant or toddler sees another child with food or drink or in the arms of a favorite adult, it may trigger a desperate need. Licht and colleagues noticed this among the fourteen-month-olds they observed (Licht, Simoni, and Perrig-Chiello, 2008).

Martha saw that Mack was drinking from a sippy cup and decided that she needed a sippy cup and a drink as well. Since Martha was not thinking about Mack owning or possessing the cup, she reached up and took the sippy cup out of Mack's mouth. Mack grabbed it right back when he saw his beloved sippy cup disappear into Martha's hands.

When Martha saw the other child drink, the cup may have reminded Martha that she likes to drink, too. When we understand Martha's motivation and help her express it—"Martha, are you thirsty, too? Would you like your own cup to drink from? You and Mack can each have your own cups"—we can help her meet her need.

Toddler Conflict

Sometimes it feels like all the conflicts among toddlers are about who will possess a toy. However, the goals of the child may be more complex than that. The toddler may want to imitate the action of another child or join in play with an interesting toy. The toddler may try to reach in to touch a toy that another child has and may be very surprised when the other toddler protests. Whatever the motivation, we know that younger children can be insistent, persistent, and demanding when they "need" a toy. We know well the child who resolutely hangs on to his toy and screeches as another child tries to take it. We are also familiar with a child who escalates conflict by using a well-directed blow to another child's arm to get him to release a desired toy. Fortunately for caring adults, insistence decreases as children develop and learn to use explanations, justifications, and conciliatory behaviors such as yielding, compromising, and negotiating (Chen et al., 2001).

Remember, too, that the social nature of conflicts often means that there is more to a conflict than just two children desiring the same toy or wanting to sit on the same pillow. Rather, the children may just want to be social. As they learn new ways of engaging other children, conflicts will decrease. Let's look more closely at the reasons that conflicts occur with toddlers.

Exploration

Just as with infants, the need to explore contributes to conflicts among toddlers. However, toddlers are exploring more quickly than infants. As they learn to walk, they may fall on another child. As they move quickly around a room, they may spot another child with an attractive toy that they want to explore. They may desire the toy or they may want to socialize with the child.

When toddlers are exploring, conflicts occur even when there are duplicates of toys that are easily accessible to the children. Imagine a toy car sitting silently on the floor. Now imagine that same toy car moving back and forth and making noises in the hands of another child. Which one would you want? A toy can suddenly become incredibly valuable and necessary to a second child because the first child has it and is playing with it. Although having duplicate toys does help prevent conflicts, to a toddler who is exploring, a toy in the hand is worth two on the floor.

Sophia sees Olivia across the room with an attractive doll in her arms, cuddling it to her neck and making soft sounds in its ear. Sophia runs as fast as her legs can carry her, but Olivia sees her coming and holds the doll in a tight embrace. Sophia begins to tug at the leg of the doll.

Young children need to explore, and their curiosity drives their learning. We want to support this critical desire to learn. When Abigail is exploring and happens upon Jazmin with an exciting toy, we can comment positively on Abigail's curiosity. We might then say to Abigail, "Jazmin has an interesting toy. What toy would you like to play with?" Look with Abigail to help her find an interesting toy, too. To encourage Abigail and Jazmin to play together, you may need to stay with them to facilitate taking turns with the toys.

Interrupted Activity, Intrusion on Play and Personal Space, and Resistance

Katie crawls over to Christopher. Christopher is inspecting a box with a lid from all sides and is very engaged in the activity. Katie seemingly does not notice Christopher's hand on the toy or doesn't recognize the significance of his hand. Katie quickly grabs the box. Christopher yowls and cries, likely because Katie interrupted his very important task of examining the box.

As with infants, a common cause for conflict is one child feeling interrupted when another child's need to explore interferes with the first child's need to complete a task. Toddlers are often appropriately focused when they are figuring out how a toy or other object works.

With older toddlers, there may be resistance toward other children who try to enter their play. Interruptions may interfere with the flow of play, a storyline, or just two friends who prefer to play with each other.

Mason and Elijah love to play with each other. When Isaac tries to join them, Mason and Elijah yell, "No!" Isaac starts to cry.

One child's intrusion on another's space can also cause conflict.

One toddler is tucked by the side of the teacher as she reads a story to the group. Another toddler plops down on the teacher's lap without looking back. The first toddler begins to protest the interruption and interference of the child, who is now blocking the first child's view and his closeness to the teacher.

Conflicts may occur over who gets to sit close to a desired adult. Older infants and toddlers may push other children to move them from the lap of a favorite teacher who is sitting on the floor. There may also be desired real estate in the room. For example, a small cubby might invite a toddler to snuggle into the space.

Other young children may have a hard time waiting for the first toddler to exit the valued territory.

There also may be resistance to hurtful or aggressive behaviors from other children. The purpose of resistance is often to defend one's own body or space or that of a friend.

Angel sits quietly on a child-size couch inspecting a book. Brianna climbs up on the couch and grabs Angel's arm very tightly. Brianna yells, "Book mine!" Angel shouts, "No, mine!"

Brianna is both invading Angel's space and hurting Angel's body. Young children need help understanding how to gently share space and objects without using their bodies aggressively to get what they want.

Dominance

Zion often toddles over to Mateo and grabs his toys away. Mateo either cries or runs away as if fearful of Zion. We might conclude that Mateo experiences Zion as dominant.

Toddlers who continuously prevail in conflicts with other toddlers, while using power techniques rather than negotiation strategies, may be considered dominant. Toddlers who are physically stronger, more mature, more cognitively advanced, more goal directed, and who have more physical and social experience in a group setting are more likely to be dominant over peers (Hawley and Little, 1999; Licht et al., 2008). Who is dominant depends on who is playing. Zion is dominant when playing with Mateo; however, when Zion is playing with Isabel, Isabel is dominant. We will want to observe this dynamic between peers very carefully. If Zion is dominant with all the children in the room and uses hurtful tactics to gain access to toys, then we will want to facilitate Zion's perspective-taking skills. If Mateo always seems to be a victim of a dominant child, then we will want to help Mateo gain confidence and the language to use with the child who always controls their play together.

Object Use, Possession, and Ownership

This is one of the most common causes of conflict among young children. Children of all ages argue over who will use a toy at times. However, children ages eighteen months to three years are only beginning to develop an understanding of the difference between possession and ownership. These concepts require higher cognitive skills. A child might possess a toy but not own the toy. A child might own a toy but not possess it at the moment.

Liam holds the ball tightly. Ethan approaches and leans toward the toy. Liam pulls the ball back quickly, and Ethan begins crying loudly.

When infants or toddlers do not yet understand possession, they quickly give up a toy that they are playing with when they lose interest. When they begin to understand possession and ownership, they often want the toy that they played with an hour ago, even if they put the toy down to go have a snack. They may especially want it if another child is now playing with it. The toy looks so exciting now in the hands of another child.

Most children between twenty-four and thirty months understand ownership and claim their toys by saying, "Mine." They are more likely to understand that a child can "own" a toy, and they are willing to give that toy back to the owner when the owner wants it (Ross, Friedman, and Field, 2015). When they say *mine*, they are more likely to also say *yours* and begin sharing with a friend (Hay, 2006). You will find strategies for helping children understand these challenging concepts in the next chapter.

Self-Regulation Challenges

Most young children have difficulty controlling their emotions, attention, effort, and behavior at times. Their brains are still maturing. They also differ in their ability to delay gratification. Some toddlers can stop themselves from taking an attractive toy out of another child's hands, while other children have difficulty inhibiting their behavior.

Language predicts self-regulation among toddlers—especially the size of their vocabulary (Vallotton and Ayoub, 2011). Toddlers control and express their emotions more easily when interacting with peers if they have words to use. A twenty-one-month-old toddler received a bite on the arm when in her toddler room. She ran to show her teacher and then, without teacher prompting, ran back to the child who bit her and said, "No, friend!" She exclaimed, "No!" while still calling the other child her friend. Her language skills helped her use words instead of biting back.

The Reason May Not Be Clear

Even when we try to think from their perspectives, we do not always know what children are thinking when they are engaged in conflict. The next best option is to observe to try to figure out what children are trying to accomplish. Are they expressing a need or are they upset because they were focusing on how a toy works? Observing will help adults understand how to help children find solutions. See Table 6 for a summary of development and learning by ages.

Table 6: Conflict Development and Learning

Age	Behaviors and Skills
4–8 months	Infants may interact with peers with their whole bodies, rolling into them, crawling over them, licking or sucking on them, or sitting on them. They are using all of their senses to investigate.
8–12 months	• Sitting infants may poke, push, or pat another baby to see what that other infant will do. They often look very surprised at the reaction that they get. • Conflicts occur because infants need to explore, are objecting to interrupted activity, and realize awakened needs (Licht, Simoni, and Perrig-Chiello, 2008). • Because infants this age are more goal oriented than younger infants, they may push another infant's hand away from a toy or crawl over another baby to get a toy.
12–18 months	• Toddlers communicate using their bodies (Løkken, 2000ab; Porter, 2003). • Toddlers may touch the object that a peer holds. This may be a positive initiation and interactive skill (Eckerman, Whatley, and McGehee, 1979). However, this may lead to conflicts. • Young toddlers are on the move. For example, in six hours, toddlers take approximately 14,000 steps, walk 46 football fields, and have 100 falls when they start to walk (Adolph et al., 2012). Because they are learning to balance and control their bodies as they walk and because they have so many falls, they may create conflict when they bump or fall into other children. • Conflicts occur because infants need to explore and will often object to interrupted activity (Licht, Simoni, and Perrig-Chiello, 2008).

Age	Behaviors and Skills
18–24 months	• Children are only beginning to understand that others have preferences different from their own and are learning how to take the perspective of another person (Astington and Edward, 2010). • Attractive toys may contribute to conflict. If there is only one, more than one child will want to play with it. It is difficult for toddlers to wait their turn. • Toddlers begin saying *mine* and *yours*. Children who began saying *mine* between eighteen and twenty-four months of age are more likely to say *yours* and share at twenty-four months (Hay, 2006). • Toddlers are still learning the differences among the concepts *take turns*, *ownership*, *possession*, *sharing*, and *giving*. • Pushing, shoving, grabbing, and hitting may occur as children struggle over "mine for as long as I want it" and "yours, but I want it, too." • Toddlers may have conflicts over small toys more than over large, unmovable objects. Children this age may intuit that larger toys are for more than one child to play with at a time (DeStefano and Mueller, 1982; Løkken, 2000b). • Children can resist with all their might when another child tries to take a toy. • Children can focus intently on completing a task, such as putting blocks into a container or placing rings on a toy. They may protest when they are interrupted. • Conflicts play a positive role in peer development as children learn that others have ideas that are different from their own and that negotiation needs to occur (Chen, et al., 2001; Eckerman and Peterman, 2001; Shantz, 1987).
24–36 months	• Many older toddlers now understand the difference between ownership and possession (Fasig, 2000); however, it is still difficult for them to control their urge to play with an attractive toy that another child has. • Children twenty-four to thirty months old understand the concept of *ownership*. They say *mine* to items they own and *yours* to items other children own (Ross, Friedman, and Field, 2015). • There is a reduction in conflict over objects (Chen, 2001). • Children use many strategies during conflicts (Hay, 2006; Hay et al., 2011). They might insist, reason, offer alternative proposals, compromise, ignore, request an explanation, or use physical force (Chen, 2001, 2003). They raise their voices, talk faster, and emphasize certain points (Brenneis and Lein, 1977). • One child's dominance over another can occur (Hawley and Little, 1999). • Biting occurs for many reasons, a primary one being that children are learning to "use their words" and take another person's perspective (Wittmer and Petersen, 2017).

Influences on the Nature of Conflicts

There are many influences on the nature of conflicts. They include children's attachment history, temperament, and gender. Conflicts are *relational*, differing depending on the relationships that children have with each other, and *situational*, occurring in a context and influenced by the opponent's previous strategies.

Attachment History and Parents' Responsiveness

A child's attachment history can influence whether he is more likely to engage in conflicts. Children with a secure attachment history and responsive family members, compared to children with an insecure attachment history, are more likely to enjoy more harmonious peer relationships (Groh et al., 2014; Hedenbro and Rydelius, 2014; Kochanska and Kim, 2012, 2013; McElwain et al., 2008). They have experienced responsiveness, sensitivity, more positive emotions, turn-taking interactions, and affection. They expect to experience the same with peers and can display more of these characteristics themselves. Children with insecure attachment histories may be more on guard around peers, expecting that others will be intrusive or unfriendly. These children may also be more aggressive or anxious and have more difficulty regulating their emotions than peers who have experienced secure attachment relationships.

Temperament

The temperament of the child influences peer relationships. Children who have lively and exuberant temperaments and also have difficulty with self-regulation may be in the middle of a group of peers, laughing, swinging toys around, and generally having a good time (Dennis, Hong, and Solomon, 2010). They may be more likely to bump into other children and grab toys that they need for their play. Children who are fearful or shy may withdraw from other children and feel uncomfortable when another child invades their territory. Teachers who are sensitive to each child's temperament can support each child's peer relationships.

Some children are emotionally reactive. They may be more sensitive and respond to people, noise, conflict, and aggression in more complex ways than other children do. They cry more easily, yell more loudly, or withdraw more quickly. For example, young children who have experienced their parents fighting and being aggressive to each other are more fearful when they face conflicts with other children (Davies et al., 2012).

Gender Differences

Boys do not seem to be involved in more conflicts than girls. However, their approaches to conflict may differ from girls' approaches. In one observed group of twenty-one-month-olds, only 35 percent of all the children used force. Force could be either instrumental (tugging on a toy) or bodily (striking out at the body of another child). Instrumental force seemed to lead to positive interactions between peers, while bodily force more likely led to negative conflicts. Boys and girls used instrumental force equally to obtain a toy. However, older toddler boys used more bodily force than did girls (Hay et al., 2011). If you see children using bodily force during conflicts, you will want to support the language development, self-regulation, and perspective-taking skills of the children.

Relationships and Situations

Conflicts differ depending on the history of relationships that children have with each other, the situation, and the strategies that children use.

> Kari wants the bright-colored basket that Thomas is waving in the air. It looks so much more attractive than the one she has in her hand. She walks over, grabs the basket, and runs away. Thomas stands looking forlorn and confused. Later Thomas runs across the room and grabs a doll out of Kari's hands.

Conflicts are relational. That is, conflicts differ depending on the relationships that children have with each other. Children who have had a conflictual relationship will probably continue to clash with each other unless there is adult guidance. The quality of the relationship and the history of the relationship between Kari and Thomas influence how they behave with each other. Very young children often learn to avoid children who begin conflicts.

Adam, a toddler in a program, seemed to be the toddler whom all the other toddlers avoided because he often hit them when he came close. The other toddlers in the room based their actions (moving away when Adam came near) on past relational experiences with him.

Adam's favorite adults explored why Adam hit other children so much and found ways, through loving relationships, to help him learn alternative ways of being with his peers.

Conflicts also are situational and influenced by the opponent's previous strategies. They occur in a context. With toddlers, the outcome of a prior conflict often affects the next conflict, and the child who lost the prior conflict is more likely to initiate the next one (Hay and Ross, 1982). Preschool children seem ready to respond in kind to their opponent's strategy (Thornberg, 2006). If an opponent during a conflict was aggressive, the other child responded with aggression. If the opponent was not aggressive, then the other child rarely used aggressive strategies. As a teacher, when you observe what seems like a child initiating a conflict, he or she may be reacting to a previous conflict. Conflicts among young children are much more complex than we have thought.

Sam and Bridger play with blocks while sitting very close together. Sam eyes a piece on Bridger's structure that would complete his block train. With a quick grab, he pries it from Bridger's structure and places it on his own. Obviously upset, Bridger whines and declares loudly to Sam, "Mine!" As Sam ignores his pleas, Bridger tries a different tactic. He raises his voice and declares, "I need that," but the words do not have their intended effect on Sam. Finally, Bridger appeals to a teacher nearby, saying, "Teacher, Sam took my block." As the teacher approaches, Sam quickly throws the piece back to Bridger.

In this example, one child initiated conflict and the other child responded by using a variety of strategies. As children grow older, they use more sophisticated ways to get objects they want.

Both younger and older toddlers have a repertoire of conflict behavior that they use. They use an amazing number of creative ways to oppose other children. For example, suppose Hannah picks up a toy that is near Carlita, and Carlita gets upset. Carlita might oppose Hanna by emphatically saying no, or she might give a reason such as, "It's mine." Carlita might propose an alternative such as, "Your car is over there." Carlita might use *postponement*: "Later you can play with it." She may try to convince Hannah that she already has a "good-enough" toy and need not try to snatch the car. Carlita may justify her actions by talking about her own needs and desires. She could provide a justification while admonishing Hanna with "Don't take my toy. That's my favorite car."

Children may also use two other types of strategies: *subordinate behavior*—crying, withdrawing, and yielding—and *conciliatory behavior*—cooperative

From Biting to Hugging: Understanding Social Development in Infants and Toddlers

propositions, apologies, symbolic offers, and sharing of objects (Chen, 2003). They also could seek adult help by tattling, whining, or simply by asking for help. Young children may use *stylistic tactics* (Shantz, 1987), such as raising their voices, talking faster, and emphasizing certain points to indicate "absolute fortissimo" or absolute determination to win. They may insist, ignore, request an explanation, or use physical force (Hay et al., 2011). The list below summarizes the strategies that toddlers might use when conflicting with another child.

- They refuse: "No."

- They claim possession and provide justification: "It's mine."

- They propose an alternative: "Your car is over there."

- They use postponement: "Later you can play with it."

- They talk about their own needs and desires: "I need it now."

- They reason with the other child: "You have a good toy."

- They tell the teacher: "She took my car."

- They insist that the other child give them a turn or a toy: "You can't have it."

- They use subordinate behavior, such as withdrawing, crying, yielding, or whining.

- They use conciliatory behavior, such as cooperative propositions, apologies, symbolic offers, and sharing of objects.

- They use stylistic tactics, such as raising their voices, talking faster, and emphasizing certain points to indicate "absolute fortissimo" or absolute determination to win.

- They ignore the other child.

- They request an explanation: "Why do you want it?"

- They use force.

Toddlers have learned a surprising number of tactics to use in conflict. It will be fun for you to watch toddlers to see which of these strategies they use. You will want to help children use some of these strategies, such as using sign language or words to use postponement—"Not now"—and justifying why they need a toy or a blanket.

As children grow, they may learn to solve more of their own conflicts and solicit assistance from teachers more often (Chen et al., 2001). Both strategies represent increased developmental knowledge about their own skills, how teachers might assist them, and greater understanding of self and other. Children are constantly learning when they are engaged in conflict with peers. With supportive adults, there is immense value in conflicts for children's development.

• • •

Conflict happens when a child resists another child's actions, protests what another child is doing or saying, or retaliates for a perceived wrong. With the right kind of support from caring and responsive adults, children learn about self and other, emotions, empathy, self-regulation, cognitive and communication skills, and how to be social and prosocial.

Infants' conflicts occur because of simple exploration, interrupted activity, and awoken needs. Toddlers conflict because of exploration, interrupted activity, dominance, object use, and self-regulation challenges. Sometimes the reasons for conflict may not be clear.

Attachment history, temperament, and gender differences influence the nature of conflicts. The history of children's relationships with each other and the strategies that infants and toddlers have learned also influence the type of conflicts that occur.

Chapter SEVEN

Strategies for Supporting Children
in Resolving Peer Conflicts

Strategies That Make a Difference

How adults view and handle the conflicts of infants and toddlers influences whether children learn new and beneficial interaction strategies or whether they continue to use unhelpful, harmful conflict strategies. In earlier chapters, we highlighted the importance of positive, caring, responsive, and affectionate adult-child relationships for children's emotional and social learning. These aspects of a program reduce conflicts and support children when they happen. As we think about peer conflicts, we want to remember that teachers support children's healthy and successful interactions with peers when the adult approach is relationship based, emotionally available, and trustworthy. It is important for children's well-being that teachers emphasize emotional and social development every day in every way.

There are beneficial adult strategies that respect children's desires to be social and prosocial, support their learning abilities, and enhance optimal emotional and social development during peer conflicts. An initial strategy for teachers to use is to reflect with their team and with parents what they want children to learn and how they want them to act with others.

Reflect, Observe, and Document

Reflecting on your team's goals for children and your attitudes and theories about conflict can make a difference in how you handle conflicts. Thoughtful observations help teachers understand children's goals. Documentation helps teachers, children, and parents appreciate the competencies and learning of young children who engage in conflicts.

Caring adults strive for children to become helpful, comfort others, and cooperate with peers. These are primary goals for infants and toddlers. These are skills that are important for success into adulthood. We want young children to have healthy connections to others and a strong sense of belonging. Before they use strategies, reflective teachers ask whether these strategies meet other goals that are important for young children.

- Does the strategy help all children feel secure, safe, and protected?
- Does the strategy model loving ways—how to comfort, share, feel and show empathy, and express emotions in healthy ways?
- Does the strategy help all children feel a sense of attachment and belonging with the adult and other children?
- Does the strategy help the child reflect on her feelings and learn how to express them?
- Does the strategy help the child learn that others may have feelings and perspectives different from their own?
- Does strategy support and/or restore positive, caring relationships between children?

An affirmative to these questions indicates that responsive adults are using strategies that support young children in becoming emotionally and socially competent.

Thoughtful teachers and families reflect on their own attitudes about conflict. If adults understand that conflicts are an important part of young children's social learning, they will approach conflicts with a supportive attitude. Rather than becoming anxious and immediately separating children during conflict, adults will make sure children have opportunities to learn valuable negotiation, problem-solving, justification, and other conflict-resolution skills.

Adults may consider how they respond to conflicts from a variety of approaches, but all strategies should aim to use conflicts as an opportunity to support blossoming social skills. Research and models from developmental psychologists can inform your methods, and although foundational theories differ slightly, the overall idea is that children are learning from the adults and peers around them how to engage in conflict and negotiate social interactions. You might use a relationship-based approach, as explained by researcher Robert Hinde, in which a teacher's primary goal is to enhance relationship-building skills among infants and toddlers (Hinde, 1992). In this method, teachers are always looking for ways to support children's relationships as they help the children negotiate conflict. A sociocultural model, which follows the research of Lev Vygotsky, says children learn conflict resolution strategies from adults, who are more expert, and from their peers (Vygotsky, 1978, 1987). Social interactions are what teach children about relationships, with adult interactions leading the way. You may also approach early childhood conflict from Jean Piaget's cognitive model (Piaget, 1936/1953), which puts an emphasis on developmental stages as children actively construct their knowledge about social relationships during conflicts. They need experience with conflicts to learn how to negotiate them, but they also need the developmental abilities to process this information. Or teachers may put a particular focus on observation and modeling. Psychologist Albert Bandura's social cognitive model says that with observational learning, children watch others closely and imitate ways to solve their social problems (Bandura, 1989).

> "Instead of trying to avoid and prevent disputes, why not use them as opportunities to help children develop strategies for the peaceful resolution of differences with others?" (Chen, 2003)

As always, teachers' strategies are individualized. When adults intervene, they should do so in strategic ways that support learning among the "disputants" (Bayer et al., 1995) and take into consideration the capabilities of the specific children engaged in the conflict. One child withdraws in the face of another infant's shriek during tussles with toys. Another child jumps into the fray with a fountain of words or a cascade of movements. These individual and cultural styles of handling conflict will influence teachers' strategies. Sometimes observation of the conflict is a first step for teachers. However, as two toddlers yell about who had a doll first, it is difficult for a teacher not to immediately intervene, especially if the teacher knows one of the toddlers likes to bite when she is frustrated. As children develop, however, if we can stop, watch, and ask first, children's ability to resolve their own conflicts will improve.

Watch first, if children aren't aggressive. We need to give children a chance to solve their own conflicts. When researcher Dora Chen and colleagues observed two-, three-, and four-year-olds, one-fourth of two-year-olds resolved their own conflicts, while one-half of four-year-olds were able to do so (Chen et al., 2001). Too much teacher intervention, as well as intervention that happens too quickly, may not give the children an opportunity to use increasingly sophisticated conflict-prevention and resolution strategies. Observing the conflict if children are not harming each other, themselves, or the environment gives children an opportunity to learn that other children's perspectives and feelings may be different from their own.

Researcher Jessica Sommerville and colleagues found that toddlers as young as twelve to fifteen months old will notice and expect a fair distribution of resources (Sommerville et al., 2013). Lead researcher Julia Ulber also found that older toddlers eighteen to twenty-four months old are able to divide resources among themselves. When given a group of marbles, older toddlers divided them equally 50 percent of the time. When one toddler received three marbles out of a machine and his partner received only one marble, the lucky child gave up one or more marbles to the unlucky child one-third of the time (Ulber et al., 2015). We want to give toddlers a chance to share by observing first instead of instructing.

Toddlers in one group care setting were rarely allowed to engage in conflict without adult interference. Adults determined the solution in 91 percent of all toddler conflicts—without involving the toddlers (DaRos and Kovach, 1998). When adults routinely directed the action and prevented toddlers from engaging in conflict resolution, they prevented toddlers from trying out different strategies.

In a different program observation, teacher interruptions in thirteen-month-olds' conflicts actually led to more negative peer interactions at nineteen months. Researchers Shannon Williams, Lenna Ontai, and Ann Mastergeorge concluded, "The rate at which caregivers interrupt infants' early peer interactions appears to have lasting negative effects on peer sociability six months later" (Williams, Ontai, and Mastergeorge, 2007). Although it is challenging for adults to move close but give children an opportunity to solve their conflict, this may be one of the most important strategies to try.

We know that toddlers often need a teacher to support their beginning ability to self-regulate strong emotions and understand other children's feelings. However, adults' constant intervention can interfere with young children's peer relationships. An interruption involves the teacher using a behavior, vocalization, or facial expression that causes a child to turn away from peers and focus on the adult. When adults interrupt toddler peer interactions, they may be negatively influencing peer sociability.

Observing helps us understand children's goals. Observing over time helps teachers and parents understand the goals and strategies of children and their reactions to them. Observing and documenting children's actions can help an adult see a behavior in a different way. Elly Singer and Maritta Hännikäinen (2002) observed teacher's strategies when two- to three-year-old children in Dutch and Finnish child-care centers conflicted over territory. They found that, for example, when two-year-olds try to enter other children's play, the peers usually reject them. Instead of giving up, young children often nonverbally stay close, circle around, and then try again. Singer and Hännikäinen pointed out that, by giving in, the child who wants to enter the play shows respect; by staying close, the child learns about the other children's activity; and by trying again, the child shows her interest. Too often we feel a need to intervene after the child is rejected, and if so, we may have interrupted the child's showing respect for her peers and learning skills for social cooperation. Observation and analysis of the documentation help us see these situations with a new lens.

Documenting the richness of peer interaction and then reflecting on these observations lead to adults seeing behaviors with new eyes. Infant and toddler development is fascinating when viewed through the lens of the child's perspective. Young children's behaviors that were seen through a negative filter can be wisely understood as progressive developmental steps toward the infant or toddler becoming socially competent.

Document peer interactions with video or photos, or ask others to record their own interactions with children. Analyze the documentation with other staff and family members to see the action from the children's perspectives and determine what type of teacher support the children need, if any.

Observing is important; however, adults must intervene when toddlers' tussles turn to turbulence and the escalation of conflict turns to aggression. Teachers' use of relationship-building strategies reduces the likelihood of these types of altercations and scaffolds children's conflict-resolution abilities.

Use the following questions to guide your observations of children's conflict behavior.

- What are the goals of children during conflict?

- How do children's goals differ by age?

- What are the strategies that children use to initiate conflict and resist during conflict?

- What gestures and words are children using during conflicts?

- Are there children who seem dominant? Who are they dominant with? How do they show dominance?

- What are children learning during conflicts?
- Are there certain toys that seem more likely to create conflicts? If so, are there fewer conflicts if you provide duplicates of an attractive toy?
- When are there the fewest conflicts? Why do you think this happens?
- How do children solve their own conflicts?
- What strategies work best to build and restore relationships between children?

Use Adult-Child Relationship-Based Strategies

Relationship-based strategies that create and sustain both adult-child and peer relationships include building and restoring relationships, using mediation strategies, and supporting children's problem-solving skills.

Build and Restore Relationships

Adults use a variety of strategies to prevent conflicts and support children's learning when conflicts occur. Some teacher strategies, however, are much more effective than others for restoring children's relationships during and after conflict occurs. These effective strategies also teach skills that enable children to regulate their own behavior. Think about how you would handle the following situation to build a friendly relationship between two toddlers (Singer, 2002). The two toddlers, with grimacing faces, are struggling over a toy, each holding tightly to a piece of the action.

Matthew, an eighteen-month-old, is playing on the floor with a blue car. He appears to be peacefully exploring how he can make noise by spinning the car wheels with his fingers. Fifteen-month-old Hamilton looks up from across the room to see where the noise originated. He sees Matthew spin the car wheels and creeps over for a better look. Hamilton watches Matthew momentarily and then lunges for the blue car. Before Hamilton can attempt a getaway, Matthew snatches the car back with a swift yank. Startled, Hamilton expresses his loss with a long, loud wail. Matthew turns his back to Hamilton, and Hamilton cries louder.

You are the teacher who watches the scene unfold from a distance. Do you:
- remove the car that is causing the conflict between the two toddlers?
- sympathetically take sides with the child you perceive to have been victimized?
- ignore the interaction, as it is one of the numerous aggravations you learn to accept in a toddler's day?
- move in close proximity to the situation, knowing that it has not finished playing itself out?

In this case, the teacher will want to move close, knowing that the conflict may escalate again. The teacher can comment on what just happened to let the children know that she understands their feelings: "Matthew, you didn't like it when Hamilton took your toy."

"Hamilton, it made you sad when Matthew took the toy back." The teacher could then ask Matthew, who is older, if he can think of a different toy to give Hamilton. If Matthew doesn't find a toy, then the teacher could suggest a few that Hamilton might like. This helps Matthew learn about what he could do in the future when a younger child takes his toy. When Matthew hands Hamilton a toy, relationship restoration is beginning.

Relationship restoration is a key concept. Both teachers' and children's communication can occur at the *content level* and at the *relational level* (Singer et al., 2012). When children conflict over activity ideas or who has the toy, they are communicating at the *content level*—it's less about the persons involved and more about specific details of this conflict. When they communicate by ignoring or rejecting other children, they are at the *relational level*—not addressing the content of the conflict but reacting to the persons involved. When Hamilton snatched the toy and Matthew swiftly grabbed it back, the conflict was at a content level—Hamilton wanted the toy; Matthew did not want Hamilton to have it. When Matthew turned his back on Hamilton, he was rejecting Hamilton on the relational level—communicating that Hamilton's feelings are meaningless to Matthew.

A conflict has escalated into a crisis when both children are simultaneously victims and aggressors. When children reject each other at both the content and relational level, ". . . there can be no resolution until children accept each other as individuals whose feelings have to be taken into account . . . only when they accept each other's presence can they resolve their problems at the content level" (Singer, 2002).

When the teacher commented on their feelings, she was helping each child think about the other as an individual with feelings. The teacher was also using mediation rather than power strategies.

Use Mediation Strategies

Building and restoring relationships with mediation strategies teaches toddlers how to negotiate peer conflict. Adults' mediating strategies, rather than power strategies, facilitate children's learning during conflict resolution.

Two types of teacher-intervention techniques can be used when child conflict escalates: mediating strategies and high-power strategies (Singer et al., 2001). As you read the following definitions of each, think about which strategy supports child learning and caring about others.

Mediating strategies involve modification—proposing changes within the logic of children's play script, avoiding prohibition rules, and appealing to verbal expression. *High-power strategies* to restore order involve giving directives, reminders of rules, and simple nonverbal objections. A high-power strategy ignores children's perspectives and can even aggravate their conflicts (Singer et al., 2001).

Had the teacher in the Matthew/Hamilton example used a high-power strategy, such as simply removing the car, she would have interfered with relationship restoration and would have contributed to the children's lack of information and skills to handle conflict in the future. Mediating restores relationships and builds children's social skills. Mediating strategies require that teachers "use their power for and with the children and foster the development of 'shared power strategies' such as negotiating; clarifying rules and feelings; questioning; and encouraging perspective taking, compromising, and restoring a relationship after a fight" (Singer, 2002).

Mediating strategies, especially those that are children centered rather than teacher centered, build on young children's existing problem-solving skills.

With older toddlers, the teacher listens to children's viewpoints, asks them to clarify their feelings, and encourages them to express their wishes to each other. These strategies recognize the competencies of young children and affirm that their ideas and relationships are important.

Conflict resolution between two young children requires that teachers maintain positive affirmation for all the involved children, support children's perspective taking, and use mediation strategies.

Use Problem-Solving Strategies

When teachers support very young children's use of problem-solving strategies, they are viewing toddler social challenges as opportunities for children to learn. Researcher Cherie Bayer and colleagues observed the strategies that thirteen teachers used in toddler disputes. Given that, in this study, some form of opposition occurred on average every 2.6 minutes and that teachers were intervening in a toddler dispute on average every 5.3 minutes, it was important to observe the strategies that teachers used and their effectiveness with toddlers. They found that toddler teachers used three different strategies in the face of tussles that occurred in twelve hours of observation.

- Call: Summon the disputants' attention

- Stop: Use physical restraint or removal of objects

- Ask: Ask the disputing toddlers to identify the problem

Call, an attempt by the teacher to get the children's attention, did not work to encourage conflict resolution. The teachers predominantly began with *stop*, which represents high teacher control and decisions about the outcome. The *ask* process—which negotiated peer opposition, supported problem solving, was more information based, and involved

From Biting to Hugging: Understanding Social Development in Infants and Toddlers

the children more—was the most effective strategy for conflict resolution, but this strategy was used in only 10.4 percent of the episodes (Bayer, Whaley, and May, 1995).

Teachers use call and stop strategies to try to stop the conflict before it escalates. However, if we think of conflicts as opportunities for very young children to learn about relationships, then it is well worth a teacher's time to first observe and then decide when or whether to intervene and to use strategies that encourage problem solving and relationship building.

In an article that explored how teachers of toddlers can foster an environment that facilitates social problem solving in times of toddler social turmoil, Lissy Gloeckler and Jennifer Cassell (2012) emphasize that teachers should engage in problem solving *with* toddlers, not *for* toddlers. "When a teacher solves problems for toddlers, she may be speaking at the toddlers rather than with them, and the toddlers may experience little or no opportunity to respond or explain their needs."

Gloeckler and Cassell created the following list to explain the difference.

- Teacher practices when problem solving for toddlers:
  » The teacher may use distraction or redirection or may physically remove a child from the location of the problem.
  » The teacher identifies the problem and ends it quickly.
  » The teacher gives directions, warnings, and reminders; the teacher makes the decision about how the problem should be resolved.
  » The teacher is brief and uses little teacher language or allows little child language.
  » The teachers hold the responsibility to manage and solve problems. Children learn that it is the teacher's job to solve problems.

- Teacher practices when problem solving with toddlers:
  » The teacher may offer comfort and touch as appropriate and identify emotions to initiate problem solving so problem solving can occur.
  » The teacher invites discussions of the situation, describes, and asks open-ended questions.
  » The teacher invites children's participation, offers choices and alternatives, and asks the children open-ended questions about their ideas.
  » The teacher gives the child or children simple scripts for self-expression.
  » The teacher and children together hold the responsibility to manage and solve problems. Children learn to self-regulate, to problem solve, and learn strategies to take care of themselves during challenging situations.

The authors write that problem-solving strategies with toddlers begin with observing, then stating the problem, and finally asking open-ended questions to understand the problem. For example, if two children want the same truck, the teacher offers comfort and asks the children to tell her what they want. Asking helps the adult discover the goals of the children. Both children may say, "Mine," or, "I had it first." The teacher may also state the problem: "Both of you want to play with the blue truck." The teacher then invites the children to think of a solution. If children cannot do this, then the teacher offers choices for the children.

Although these problem-solving strategies take more time when teachers solve problems with children, they encourage children's recognition and expression of emotions, their ability to think about solutions, their ability to regulate their own behavior, and relationship restoration.

Create a Caring Community—Environments and Responsive Program Planning

Rushing children through the day, putting too many children together in one space, and an inflexible schedule all contribute to increased conflict among infants and toddlers. To reduce conflict, create a schedule that responds to the needs of infants and toddlers. Feed infants and help them sleep on their own schedules. Toddlers, on the other hand, thrive with more organized routines of "hello" time, eating, sleeping, indoor and outdoor play time, and "goodbye" time. However, teachers of these age groups must remain flexible to meet the needs of young children who may need more holding one day and, on the next day, may want to continue eating after the other children are finished with their lunch "because their tummies aren't full yet." This kind of responsive care—that trusts children to tell you what they need—gives children a sense of efficacy and control and helps them to trust their own feelings of hunger, need for rest, and desire for companionship.

Because the possession of objects and intrusion on personal space are the two most likely causes of

"Children's territorial conflicts stem from a classic problem in child care centers—the dilemma of children wanting to play together while also needing privacy. The data suggest that teachers indirectly influence the occurrence and seriousness of such conflicts by their organization of time, space, and material" (Singer and Hannikainen, 2002).

conflict (Hay et al., 2011), teachers can provide enough toys that are in good repair for all the children and can display them in attractive ways. Have duplicates of some toys to encourage complex play among children. Create cozy corners in the room where a child who needs to focus without intrusion can go.

Support Families

Families often seek help for how to handle their children's conflicts. Family workshops or brochures on the value of conflicts and the importance of teaching children problem-solving skills can be beneficial to parents. Help family members understand that relationship restoration and children learning from conflicts are priorities. Short videos and documentation of children's conflicts, with an analysis of children's goals, help family members understand that when a young child takes a toy from another child, it is most likely not an aggressive act and can have many meanings, including "I want to play with you." Reflecting on children's goals helps adults not react to conflict, but rather to figure out what the meaning of the conflict is to the children themselves.

Summary of Strategies

Strategies that make a difference include teachers' reflection and observation. Teachers and families together will want to revisit their goals for the children and reflect on their attitudes about conflict. Observing conflicts, rather than intervening immediately (unless aggression is involved), is critically important to understand toddlers' goals and to give toddlers an opportunity to solve problems with each other. Adult-child relationship-based strategies include building and restoring relationships, using mediation strategies and using problem-solving strategies with children.

A caring community that provides a relaxed environment, a flexible schedule, a small teacher-child ratio, duplicate toys in good repair, and cozy corners is vitally important for preventing conflicts and supporting amicable solutions. Support the families of children by providing family workshops or brochures on the value of conflicts and the importance of teaching children problem-solving skills. Help family members understand that relationship restoration and children learning from conflicts are important and build skills that will help children now and in the future. Share short videos and documentation of children's conflicts to help families understand children's goals with their peers and the strategies they've learned to negotiate and cooperate with peers.

- Reflect, observe, and document:
  - » Revisit the team's and families' goals for the children and yourselves.
  - » Reflect on your own and on your team's attitudes about conflict. Conflict has value for children's learning if adults use mediating and problem-solving strategies and support children in thinking of the other.
  - » Thoughtfully observe. Observing helps us understand children's goals.

- » Watch first, if children aren't using aggression.
- » Understand all the reasons that conflict occurs, so that you can take the perspective of the child.

- Use adult-child relationship-based strategies:
  - » Build and restore relationships. Relationship restoration is a key concept.
  - » Use mediation strategies by proposing changes within the logic of children's play script, avoiding prohibition rules, and appealing to verbal expression.
  - » Teach children the meaning of words and concepts such as *mine, yours, his, hers, owner,* ownership, and possession.

- Use problem-solving strategies:
  - » Offer comfort and touch as appropriate.
  - » Identify emotions to initiate problem solving or so problem solving can occur.
  - » Invite discussions of the situation, describe, and ask open-ended questions about the situation.
  - » Invite children's participation, offer choices and alternatives, and ask the children open-ended questions about their ideas.
  - » Give the child or children simple scripts for self-expression.
  - » Along with the children, hold the responsibility to manage and solve problems. Children learn to self-regulate, how to problem solve, and learn strategies to take care of themselves during challenging situations.

- Create a caring community:
  - » Provide a relaxed environment.
  - » Provide a responsive and flexible schedule.
  - » Ensure a small teacher-child ratio.

- » Provide enough toys that are in good repair.

- » Provide duplicates of some toys.

- » Provide cozy corners where there may be less intrusion on space.

- Support families:

- » Provide family workshops or brochures on the value of conflicts and the importance of teaching children problem-solving skills.

- » Help family members understand that relationship restoration and children learning from conflicts are priorities.

- » Share short videos and documentation of children's conflicts with an analysis of children's goals to help family members understand that children's actions can have many meanings.

From Biting to Hugging: Understanding Social Development in Infants and Toddlers

Chapter EIGHT

Children Who Feel Particularly Challenged
with Peer Relationships

Children from birth to three years of age are in the process of developing the social attitudes and skills that they need for harmonious interactions and conflict negotiation. Because these skills develop in the early years, all young children sometimes find peer interactions challenging. Yet, some children who experience social delays or disabilities find peer interactions challenging most of the time.

The quality of a child's peer relationships provides a window into the child's sense of well-being. Children's characteristics, such as temperament, their experiences with relationships, and the quality of the environment they experience, all play a part in whether infants and toddlers feel challenged by peer relationships (Dollar and Buss, 2014; Heberle et al., 2014; Waller et al., 2015).

Challenges with Relationships Begin Early

Cara does not want to be touched by her peers. She moves away whenever a peer comes near. Lonnie squeezes herself into the tiny space between the block shelf and the puzzle shelf. Langston whimpers when another toddler takes a toy from him, and Ariel often hits other children for no apparent reason.

Infants and toddlers like Cara, Lonnie, Langston, and Ariel may feel sad, tired, fearful, rejected by peers, angry, frustrated, upset, disoriented, or confused. Some children may have difficulty expressing their feelings in healthy ways. Children may be irritable or may lash out at others. Some seem to want to hurt first before being hurt. Peers who anticipate scary or hurtful responses from these children may scurry away as they move through the room. Other children do not hurt others; instead, they may withdraw to a corner of the room, act fearful, refuse another child's initiation to play, cling tightly to a teacher's leg, or cry for long periods. Children who experience toxic stress, grief, abuse, neglect, or traumatic events show us how distressed they are in many of the ways just described. We have all seen these children who we know need relationship support. Teachers and family members may refer to these children as withdrawn, too shy, inhibited, aggressive, rejected or rejecting, traumatized, depressed, or grieving.

We may see signs of a child's relationship challenges early in the first year of life. Caring teachers worry about these children because they are generally not happy. With an empathetic, loving, insightful approach, teachers can help children who feel challenged move forward toward successful peer relationships. Young children's early care and learning experiences have the power to enhance and advance peer social attitudes and skills.

Understanding challenging behavior begins with an attitude of respect for what infants and toddlers reveal to us with their expressions of feelings and other behaviors. Infants and toddlers tell us they are troubled or well through their play, sleep patterns, eating, affect, body tone, cries, and words and through their approach and response to adult and peer relationships. Whether an infant or toddler feels challenged for a few minutes, hours, days, or consistently, we want to try to figure out what is happening with the child so we can help.

All infants' and toddlers' behavior has a source, meaning, and purpose. If we carefully observe, dialogue with families, and thoughtfully reflect, we will figure out how to support children as they negotiate relationship experiences. We walk with them on their pathway to social competence.

Patterns of Challenging Behavior

When we focus on infants and toddlers who find peer relationships particularly challenging, we begin to see several patterns of relating. These patterns tell us about what a child has already experienced in his young life and reveal aspects of the child's temperament. They expose young children's skills and attitudes about social relationships and the children's feelings about themselves and others. They tell us what the child is expecting from relationships. For example, a toddler who withdraws from peers is probably not expecting peer relationships to be fun, easy, or satisfying. Children's patterns of relating also tell us what they need. A two-year-old who plays

> "Babies and toddlers may be lovable in most ways, but they still can do things that are provocative" (Heitler, 2011).

roughly with peers may need sensory stimulation, nurturing, or self-regulation skills. Let's start with biting—a common and very challenging problem that adults face with infants and toddlers.

Biting Others

Biting is a serious concern of children, families, and teachers and often occurs where there are young children together. When a bite occurs, the center room or family child-care home often erupts with emotion. On the cusp of using language to express their needs, mobile infants' or toddlers' bites may convey what they cannot say with words: "I like you," "Get out of my way," or "Give me back my toy! I had it first." Biting is a major concern for teachers who want children to become prosocial members of their peer community.

Biting typically is not done to intentionally hurt another person, but rather to obtain a desired object, express frustration, move another person out of the way, or even to express affection. One of the biggest reasons that infants, toddlers, and two-year-olds bite others is that they lack other tactics to express their desires and needs. They also bite others because they

have teeth that they are learning how to use. Children bite all the time—their food, their toys, and their books. They must learn that people are not for biting.

When children are together in early care and learning programs they need support, encouragement, prompting, and relationship reestablishment strategies from sensitive and responsive adults to learn alternatives to biting.

Children may bite other people for various reasons, and understanding these reasons will help the caring adult to respond appropriately. Let's explore why young children bite and the program solutions that correspond with each reason. Reasons for biting include the following:

- Holding on and letting go

- Autonomy

- Exploration
- Teething
- A desire for peer interaction
- Cause and effect
- Imitation
- Attention
- Frustration
- Anger
- Stress and anxiety

Holding On and Letting Go

As children's muscles mature, toddlers experiment with two simultaneous ways of handling experiences: holding on and letting go. Toddlers are learning to both hold on to and let go of parents and other adults and toys, among other things. Children learn to hang on and let go with their mouths. They may want to play with other children but do not know how to

initiate and sustain interactions. So they may, at inopportune times, hang on to other children with their bites. When we recognize that biting may be a way of interacting, we can help young children learn how to initiate in positive, prosocial ways.

When young children are separating from parents, they have to "let go" of them. This is challenging for many children. They sometimes hang on to parents with cries and hugs. Help ease infant and toddler separations from their family members at the beginning of the day. If the child cries when the parent leaves, then say to the child, "You're feeling very sad. It's hard to say goodbye. Mommy will come back after nap." Empathizing, naming the child's feelings, and reminding him that he will see his parent after some concrete event will help the child feel a little better about the separation.

To give children practice with holding on and letting go of toys or other desired objects, offer opportunities such as putting blocks into containers.

Holding on and letting go appears in another area: toilet learning. Don't pressure toilet learning. Wait until the child shows that he can "let go" in other areas of life.

Autonomy

Toddlers develop autonomy as they begin doing things for themselves, making choices, needing to control, making demands of adults and the environment, wanting power, and moving out and away from adults. Biting others may help some children feel powerful. Toddlers may show control of the other person or the situation when they bite.

Toddlers must be helped to achieve a balance between their need for control and their need for loving, firm limits for their often uncontrollable urges. Allow and provide as many situations as possible when the children can choose and have power. For example, offer a choice between a red marker and a blue marker,

From Biting to Hugging: Understanding Social Development in Infants and Toddlers

the Cheerios or the Rice Krispies, or milk or no milk on their cereal. These choices may not seem like a big deal to you, but they are to a child. Give children long stretches of time to choose, explore, and learn. Toddlers who are out of control need loving adults to provide safe boundaries for them. Without limits, children can actually feel more out of control.

Exploration

Biting is a part of sensory-motor exploration. Toys, food, and people must be touched, smelled, and, of course, tasted if the toddler is to learn. Young children are sensuous creatures who learn through the use of their senses and their motoric actions on things and around things. As children explore, they often are not fully in control of their walking, running, or handling objects and may unintentionally interfere with other children's play. Children whose play has been interrupted may communicate their displeasure with bites.

Provide a variety of sensory-motor experiences in the center. Infants and toddlers should experience closely supervised play with water, paints, playdough, and sand. Give children opportunities to crawl and tumble over a variety of hard, soft, rough, and smooth surfaces. A colorful array of toys that can be mouthed and easily washed should be available. Ensure opportunities for the infants and toddlers to practice blossoming motor skills and have private spaces to concentrate on a task such as putting together a puzzle without peer intrusion.

Teething

Teething can cause an infant's or a toddler's mouth to hurt. Babies often need something or someone to gnaw on to comfort them. Provide the infant or toddler with safe teething toys. Older children can be encouraged to bite on foods and firm teething toys. Keep clean frozen cloths on hand to provide cooling relief for the teething toddler and for the child who has been bitten.

A Desire for Peer Interaction

Infants and toddlers are just beginning to learn how to engage peers in positive ways. Infants usually do not understand they hurt others when they bite them; although, older toddlers may understand this. Toddlers often do not know how to approach their peers in acceptable ways. They often express their interest by biting, pulling hair, pushing, and so on.

Children need lots of social experiences to learn how to interact with others. Take the child's hand when he reaches out to the other roughly, and say, "Touch gently. That makes him feel happy." Acknowledge a child's interest in other children by saying, "I know you like Darin. You can give him a toy." Notice and acknowledge positive peer interaction such as one child hugging another, giving a toy to another, and smiling to another.

Cause and Effect

Young children begin to investigate cause-and-effect relationships at approximately three months. It is as if a toddler thinks, "What will happen if I bite Susie? What reaction will I get?" Biting gets a reaction and usually a very strong one! The biting child often receives a loud scream from the other child and a strong response from an adult.

Provide toys that do something when the child acts on the toy. For example, when a button is pushed, a figure pops up; when a knob is turned, music plays. Sand, dirt, water, paints, blocks, and crayons allow for creative, open-ended experiences that offer many opportunities for the child to make something happen. Help children notice the positive reaction they get when they pat, hug, or give a toy to another child.

Imitation

Young children learn by imitating others, and biting is one behavior that is often learned from others. After fifteen months, toddlers will observe a behavior such as biting, store it in their memories, and perform the act later when conditions are right for it. This is called *deferred imitation*. Children who are physically punished are more likely than their peers to be aggressive with both adults and peers—especially younger, smaller peers. They learn that hitting and biting others is an acceptable way of handling their anger if they see adults responding in that way.

Children learn positive ways of interacting with others through imitation. Model loving, nurturing, sharing, polite, positive behavior for young children to imitate. Develop a repertoire of behaviors for handling children's hurtful behavior that model relationship-restoration strategies. Model talking about feelings. Use positive techniques that emphasize the perspectives of others for them to imitate. When a child wants a toy another child has, comment positively on his use of the words, "Peas [please], my turn?" so other children have the opportunity to hear the words and imitate using them.

Attention

The young child may bite others to get attention; it is true that negative attention seems to be better to many toddlers than no attention at all. Children under age three hate to be ignored. Some children may actually be receiving more attention from teachers for negative behaviors than for positive behaviors, thus continuing the cycle of negative behaviors.

At times when no biting is occurring, nurture the child who bites with positive, warm attention. This can be difficult when the adult is feeling frustrated with the little child who bites. Remember, however, that when children's positive, busy, curious, helpful, productive behaviors are noticed, the children are much more likely to behave that way more often. Break into that negative cycle of child behavior with adult positive comments and hugs for desirable behavior.

Frustration

Too many children, high adult-to-child ratios, not enough space, or just simply not getting what they want can lead children to frustrated, biting behavior. Because they are still developing regulation skills, young children may act out when they are blocked or thwarted from obtaining a desired object, food, or person.

Acknowledge the feelings of children. Say, "I know you wanted another banana. I'm sorry. I wish I could give it to you. I don't want you to get a tummy-ache." Young children may not understand all the words; however, they will understand your empathetic tone. Teach the child to say, "I feel frustrated (sad, happy)."

Take a look at your classroom environment. The environment for the young children may need to be changed before biting will decrease. Fewer children in a classroom makes a big difference in children's sense of well-being.

Anger

The young child may bite others due to feelings of anger at adults and peers because of unmet needs or because of harsh discipline techniques. A child who has cried for attention but has gone unheard or a child who is hit, slapped, yelled at, or bitten by adults may become an angry child who bites.

Meet the child's needs for loving care. Build trust with a child by being consistently responsive. Say, "I do not want you to hit. I can help you." Help the young child to develop a repertoire of behaviors for handling angry feelings. Help the child to learn how to say or use sign language to communicate *no* to another child who grabs a toy.

Stress and Anxiety

A young child may be experiencing a generalized anxiety about events happening to him or around him, such as parents' divorcing or fighting, the loss of or separation from loved ones, and so on. Anxiety may lead to the toddler biting others to relieve tension. Also, children may feel confused, emotionally wounded, and disconnected from reality.

Work with parents to determine the source of a child's stress. With the child, provide calming activities such as water or sand play. Allow the child to suck a thumb or hold a transitional object such as a blanket or stuffed animal. Provide time for one-on-one with a special adult. Rock, pat backs, and sing songs at nap time to quiet children into sleep. Play soothing lullabies. Stay close to nurture the child and help her through transition times. Talk soothingly to the child about the things going on in her life. Caring adults will need to help these children connect with their own emotions as well as others' emotions.

In the Moment When a Child Bites

When a biting incident happens, the goal is to support both children emotionally. Teach both the child who bites and the victim different strategies that are appropriate for each child's developmental level. Always use techniques that restore relationships.

If the biter did not break the skin of the other child, then calmly, kindly, and seriously do the following:

- **Ask what happened, or state the problem.** For example, say, "Kevin, you took the toy from Charley. Charley, you bit Kevin."

- **Ask about or emphasize the perspective and feelings of the child who was hurt.** Point out how the biter's behavior affected the other child. Say, "Kevin doesn't like it when you bite him. That hurt him. He's crying." Encourage the child who received the bite to tell the biter or sign *stop* or "Be nice." Emphasize the biter's feelings, too. "Charley, you seemed angry. You wanted the toy back."

- **Ask or state an alternative approach.** Teach the biting child what to do instead. "Charley, you can bite this cloth (food, biting toy) if you're angry," or "You can tell Kevin how you feel," or "Come to me, and I will help you."

- **Encourage the child who bit to think of how to help the other child feel better.** Suggest an ice pack, a favorite toy, or an adhesive bandage.

If the skin is not broken, teachers must fill out an accident report and talk with both the parents of the child who bit and the parents of the child who received the bite. If the skin of the child who was bitten is broken, ask another teacher to help so that one of you can talk to the child who bit using these strategies and one of you can attend to the bite. **Follow the protocol for your program.** Generally, if the skin is broken, the usual protocol is for the parent to take the child to a doctor and for the teacher to complete an accident report.

These are general strategies to keep in mind when dealing with biting.

- Use words or actions appropriate to a child's developmental level.

- Adults may discount the biter as a person with feelings, but that child is often as frightened as the victim. If punishment for the child who bit is harsh, the young child may nurse his own hurt rather than concentrating on helping the victim of the bite. If you punish or yell at the child or put the child in time-out, he will try to protect himself, think only of himself, likely feel ashamed, and will not be open to learning about alternatives to biting others and helping the one he has hurt.

- Observe when the biting occurs. Keep records and look for patterns. A child may bite before lunch each day because he is hungry and frustrated because he can't eat yet. Other children might bite when other children crowd around them or after a weekend without their mom.

- If one child's biting continues after several days of repeating these techniques, meet with the family and other teachers to figure out what might be causing the child to bite. Explore with the parents the reasons for biting. Then, plan together to provide consistent approaches across home and the learning program. Try a solution based on the possible reasons. Review the results with the family and teaching team. Try another strategy. Infants and toddlers deserve our best planning, caring, and teaching.

- Implement a program of time-in with an adult. Have an adult shadow the child, meet the child's emotional needs, show the child affection and encouragement, and catch him before he bites. This adult can teach him alternative behaviors, and help him learn how to be gentle or use sign language or words to express his needs.

- Have a staff meeting. Review all the reasons that young children bite and all the techniques that teachers use. Individualize strategies for a child and then work together as a team to provide caring relationships and consistency for that child.

Before parents become upset about the biting problem, hold a parent meeting or send a newsletter home to let parents know about the relationship-restoration techniques they and the staff can use. Parents need to know why young children bite, that it is a common problem whenever young children are together in a group, and that the staff should do everything possible to ensure the safety of the children. Send home a handout on why biting happens and the strategies that you use to help children who bite and the children who receive the bites. Explain the protocol for procedures when biting occurs. Many programs have decided that they will not reveal the name of the child who bit. What is your program's protocol? All programs need to create it, know it, and practice it.

More Points about Biting and Guidance

If adults bite children to "show them what it feels like," they are giving a conflicting message by saying, "No biting," while at the same time biting the children. If adults bite, they model hurtful behavior. When adults hit or bite children as punishment for biting others, children learn that biting is okay if you are bigger and stronger than the other person. Children then may be more likely to bite their peers, especially smaller ones.

Support adults in a child's life to consider the child's temperament, experiences that may be stressful for the child, their goals for the child, and strategies to achieve those goals. Help parents understand that positive discipline techniques are more effective than negative ones. Discipline is a complicated issue and one that is highly challenging to most parents. Parents who use physical punishment or other negative techniques often have positive intentions, but simply do not understand how to use alternative, positive techniques to achieve their goals.

In a national survey conducted in 2015 by Zero to Three, 77 percent of parents who spanked regularly (several times per week) said that it was not a very effective form of punishment. Sixty-nine percent of parents said that if they knew more positive parenting strategies, they would use them (Zero to Three, 2016). When adults who use negative guidance techniques with young children learn about the detrimental effects of physical punishment, name calling, shaming, or love withdrawal and learn the positive effects of giving reasons, making it clear to children how you want them to behave, and helping them take the perspective of others, they are less likely to use physical punishment to discipline their children. In one intervention program, parents were given information on the detrimental effects of spanking. This included information on how spanking one- and three-year-olds was related to their children's behavior problems, including aggression at ages three and five (Gromoske and Maguire-Jack, 2012; Lee et al., 2013). The parents who received the information spanked their children less and used other techniques more.

If a solution works, give yourself a big pat on the back. If a solution does not work, provide the time-in approach. If the child continues biting, bites viciously, or bites and then smiles, seek professional help and explore the possibility that this child needs an environment with fewer children and more one-on-one attention for a while.

(Material on biting is adapted from Wittmer and Petersen, 2017.)

Aggressive, Angry, or Defiant Behavior

Sardi, a toddler, hits other toddlers. When Mara takes a plastic plate that is in front of Sardi and then leaves the dramatic play area, Sardi picks up another plate, runs across the room, and hits Mara on the head.

In this example, the aggressive act was Sardi hitting Mara on the head. In general, aggression is defined as intentionally hurting another, either verbally or physically. But for children ages birth to three, the definition often does not include intention. It is difficult to determine intention in a young child's actions. Instead, we define physical aggression in young children as behavior that does or has the potential of causing physical harm to people, animals, or objects.

Examples of physical aggression are hitting, kicking, fighting, biting, scratching, and pinching. Aggression can be proactive or reactive. *Proactive aggression* occurs when a child initiates aggressive behavior, and *reactive aggression* occurs when a child reacts to another's aggression. However, often what we think is proactive aggression is the child reacting to another child's aggression that we didn't see. Sometimes we see only one act of the aggression.

"While researchers and other professionals used to think that aggression developed in adolescence, they now look at the infant and toddler age period as crucial for children to develop self-control and non-aggressive attitudes . . . [T]he peak age for physical aggression was not during early adulthood, adolescence, or even kindergarten, but rather between twenty-four and forty-two months after birth" (Tremblay, 2004).

When Do We See Aggression?

Experienced family members and teachers see aggressive behavior early with a few children. Many researchers also see a pattern for the onset and incidence of aggressive behavior. Physical aggression appears during the first year after birth. The beginnings of aggression—anger, hitting, and biting—have been observed as early as six months of age. Aggression becomes more frequent during the second year and reaches a peak between twenty-four and forty-two months after birth, and then decreases steadily (Tremblay, 2004). We must remember, however, that a very small percentage of children use aggression frequently (Baillargeon et al., 2007).

Reasons for Aggression

It is challenging to know how to help children who feel angry or who use aggressive behaviors frequently. It is helpful to look at some of the underlying causes and then tailor strategies to the needs of the children. There are reasons why there is an increase in aggression from twelve months to approximately thirty-six months of age (Alink et al., 2006). Children during this age period may experience anger, frustration, and the confusing feelings of becoming autonomous,

> "The toddler craves independence, but he fears desertion."
>
> —Dorothy Corkille Briggs, author and psychologist

self-directing, and independent. They are constantly striving for independence and at the same time concerned that adults won't keep them safe. They want to be very grown-up one minute and your cuddly baby the next.

They may not be able to make their needs known to adults as well as they would like. Demands on a child's behavior become greater as they age. By three years of age when aggression begins to decrease, children begin to internalize rules and values, their communication skills increase, and their negotiation and persuasive skills improve. The toddler years are crucial years for helping young children learn to express their aggressive feelings in an appropriate manner (Tremblay, 2004; Williams, Ontai, and Mastergeorge, 2007).

Children who experience attachment security (Groh et al., 2014), learn how to recognize and manage emotions in themselves and others (Lauw et al., 2014), and receive clear messages that aggression is not okay (Christopher et al., 2013) are less likely to be aggressive at age three. The following are some other factors that contribute to children using aggressive behaviors:

- **Health issues, including the need for sleep:** Young children's ability to function and control their emotions is sleep related (Miller et al., 2015). Ensuring that young children get adequate sleep is of utmost importance. Iron deficiency and lead poisoning are also two contributors to children's behavior challenges. A health check-up should be one of the first things that families should pursue if their child becomes aggressive.

- **Language needs:** In a group of almost two thousand children studied from birth to forty-one months, frequent physical aggression related specifically to receptive vocabulary deficits (Séguin et al., 2009). It can be frustrating for a child not to understand what is being said or what adults and peers want him to do. Checking a child's hearing is one of the first things that teachers and families should do. If a child's hearing is good, then your team will want to determine strategies for supporting the child's auditory and vocabulary development.

- **Experiencing stress:**

Tiesha usually was very affectionate with the other toddlers in her room in the care and learning program. After a long weekend, Tiesha seemed tired. She cried when her mother said goodbye. When Samantha accidentally stepped on Tiesha's toes, Tiesha lashed out and scratched Samantha on the arm. The next day, Tiesha bit LaBron's back as he lay on the floor. Tiesha was having a very difficult time with her peers. The teachers decided to talk with the parents to see if they knew why Tiesha seemed worried, tense, anxious, and sometimes angry.

Children may experience stress in a variety of ways. Lack of predictability in a child's life often leads to the child feeling stressed. Life changes, which can be caused by moves, deaths, changes in parent work hours, divorces, or birth of a sibling, affect children's stress levels. A neglected or abused child experiences chronic stress (Klein et al., 2013). We know that when young children experience continued and extreme stress experiences without supportive adult-child relationships, long-term detrimental effects on young children's brain development and health may result. This is because of the stress hormone cortisol that is activated in the fight-or-flight response (Center on the Developing Child, 2017d). Children may experience positive stress, with brief increases in heart rate and cortisol levels, which help children learn to cope with adversity; however, toxic stress increases the risk for stress-related disease and cognitive impairment into adulthood (Center on the Developing Child, 2017d).

Some children may experience stress in child care and learning programs.

Ariel, an eight-month-old, started the day with a smile for her teacher and her peers. She played on the floor for a while with a teacher near. But, by the end of the day in child care, Ariel was irritable and difficult to comfort. She seemed to feel stressed.

Conner, a toddler, seemed fearful around other children. As the day in child care progressed, he seemed more stressed than the other toddlers who liked to play with other children.

Infants and toddlers who are shyer and more socially fearful with their peers are more likely to experience an increase in cortisol in child-care settings. These children have a more difficult time managing their negative emotions (Watamura et al., 2003). These children may not receive the emotional support they need, thus leading to the children's (and the teachers') increased stress levels (Groeneveld et al., 2012). High quality care, a secure attachment with a teacher, and teachers who are not intrusive and overcontrolling (Gunnar et a1., 2010) result in less stress. A warm, personal emotional climate also significantly reduces infants' and toddlers' stress in child care (Watamura et al., 2009).

Children's temperaments can also influence their stress levels. Some children have difficulty being touched. Some feel more irritable than others. Some are boisterous and need active play. Considering and accommodating children's temperaments helps them learn sociable behaviors.

Teachers who form strong, affectionate relationships with the children can mediate children's stress levels (Sims et al., 2006.) This is just another reason for teachers to provide contingently responsive, developmentally effective, and affectionate care.

> "Children love and want to be loved, and they very much prefer the joy of accomplishment to the triumph of hateful failure. Do not mistake a child for his symptom."
>
> —Erik Erikson, developmental psychologist

- **Harsh caregiving or conflictual relationships:** In a study by Karen Benzies and colleagues, parent hostility and lack of warmth was found to lead to children's angry, disruptive, disorganized, and aggressive behavior (Benzies et al., 2009). Children who do not experience sensitivity, such as a parent reading a child's cues for hunger, or empathy for their distress, are less prosocial (Blandon and Scrimgeour, 2015). Young children who experience parental aggression toward them are at risk for *limited prosocial emotions* (LPE) (Waller et al., 2014). Children may be experiencing violence in their homes and toward themselves. Parents and children may be engaged in a relationship characterized by negativity, anger, and conflict. These children may have learned to avoid adults and yet feel angry because of unmet needs. They may be imitating aggressive behavior and may not be learning alternative strategies to using aggression with others.

Parents who, as children, felt alone and lonely may have difficulty providing loving care for their own children. Family depression can contribute to children's problem behaviors. Marital conflict may lead to young children feeling the tension in the home and modeling their behavior after parents who express frequent anger (Crockenberg, Leerkes, and Lekka, 2007). Families with multiple risk factors benefit from family support, home-visiting programs, community resources, and intervention programs.

The Difference between Boys' and Girls' Aggression

In a study of ten thousand Canadian toddlers, one sixth of the children were rated as highly aggressive. Most of these children were boys (Côté et al., 2006). These children continued to use aggressive behaviors into their teen years. The children with high levels of aggression were more likely to be from low-income families and families where parents reported using hostile and punitive parenting strategies. Another study of children ages seventeen to twenty-nine months found that 5 percent of boys but only 1 percent of girls used aggressive behaviors frequently (Baillargeon et al., 2007).

Why might boys be more aggressive than girls? Boys may be expected to be more aggressive by societal norms. Parents' violent behavior with each other seems to result in aggressive behavior more often in boys than in girls. (Tailor and Letourneau, 2012). More research is needed to illuminate under what conditions girls or boys may be more aggressive. Meanwhile, prosocial environments and nurturing solutions work for both boys and girls.

Children Who Use Aggressive Behavior Need Help Now

Aggressive behavior is a symptom of a child's distress. We cannot ignore aggressive behavior. One study of approximately three hundred infants who exhibited anger by hitting, biting, and flailing out at people at just six months of age predicted toddlers' aggressive behavior at twenty months and thirty-three months (Hay et al., 2010; Hay et al., 2014). Another study concluded that children at risk for aggressive and disruptive behavior can be spotted at fifteen months, based on their interactions with their peers in a program setting (Deynoot-Schaub and

Riksen-Walraven, 2006). Examples of negative peer interactions are hitting, pushing, pulling, or kicking other children; taking away objects; and verbal or nonverbal sounds of protest.

We also know that toddler aggression predicts academic achievement at school age (Brennan et al., 2012) and at age twelve (Campbell et al., 2006). A study by Soo Hyun Rhee and colleagues found that toddlers' disregard for others' pain at fourteen to thirty-six months predicted antisocial behavior in middle childhood and adolescence (Rhee, et al., 2013). These were toddlers who hit, ran, showed anger, laughed menacingly, or were judgmental—"That was stupid"—when their twin or mother experienced pain. It seems we must act immediately if an infant or toddler seems more aggressive or disregards others' distress more than other children do. However, since even low levels of aggression that continue from toddlerhood through childhood are a concern for future social and academic achievement, the toddler years are key years for helping children learn alternative strategies to aggression.

We do know that socially competent children are aggressive at times and even that aggression is an aspect of social competence (Vaughn et al., 2003; Williams et al., 2007). One can imagine the very sociable toddler who is always in the middle of the action and at times may push or hit another toddler. Intense and proactive aggression, however, is of concern and requires intervention, as does hostile aggression. Children who frequently misinterpret their peers' intentions as negative also need additional support from adults to help them learn to interpret other children's behavior as benevolent or neutral and not to be overly sensitive. These young children may be on guard to ensure their own safety.

Anger and Defiance

Jada, a two-year-old, picked up a chair and threw it as far as her small body could when Lucia, the teacher, said that the group wasn't ready to go outside. Martina, who was playing nearby, looked up and started crying. Jada's teachers wondered why Jada often seem annoyed and sometimes furious when she couldn't do what she wanted to do immediately. The teachers decided that they needed to help Jada learn to manage her angry and defiant feelings.

Anger is a normal reaction to frustration, betrayal, or feeling threatened or attacked. It may occur as a second feeling after fear or guilt. Feeling anger is neither bad nor good. Anger can result in healthy or unhealthy behavior, depending on how the anger is expressed. Jada did not have the strategies to express her anger in healthy ways. So, she used ways that hurt others and damaged objects.

Defiance and noncompliance are typical behaviors for toddlers. These children are in a quest for greater autonomy (Baillargeon et al., 2011). However, just as with aggression, frequent and severe oppositional and defiant behaviors are not typical. We should be concerned when typical toddler noncompliance is accompanied by severe aggressive behavior.

Children who feel angry and who haven't learned nonaggressive ways to express it may hit, bite, throw

> "One of the most important developmental issues facing the toddler in the second year of life is to maintain connectedness with the caregiver while carrying his or her own inner aims and goals" (Baillargeon et al., 2010).

chairs, stomp their feet, threaten their peers, or run away. When toddlers say no and defy adult directives with hands on their hips, they are behaving normally (Baillargeon et al., 2011), but if they also hit, bite, and kick when they oppose adults and peers, then you will want to support the children's autonomy while helping them learn alternative behaviors to aggression.

Other Peer Challenges Young Children Experience

Teachers and parents worry about infants, toddlers, and two-year-olds who seem angry and behave defiantly. They feel discomfort for children who are inhibited, shy, withdrawn, and who reject other children. Caring adults know that children birth to three are just learning how to manage and express difficult emotions; however, they wonder why some children frequently have difficulty controlling their emotions and behavior and seem out of control. Teachers and parents try to figure out why some

children are rejected by their peers at such an early age. They wonder how children with autism and those who have experienced trauma and abuse express their needs. Concerned professionals strive to help these children manage and experience healthy relationships with both adults and peers. With each of these challenges, let's look at the behaviors we might see and the strategies that we can use to support children and families.

From Biting to Hugging: Understanding Social Development in Infants and Toddlers

Children Who Feel Shy, Cautious, Anxious, Inhibited, Withdrawn, Rejected, or Fearful

Lotty, a toddler, looks on with a passive face as other children play. Meghan actively avoids all the toddlers in the room, moving in the other direction when children come near her. Mark seems fearful when he must be with the other children.

Children who withdraw from other children have been considered inhibited, hiders, or social isolates. They are different from toddlers and two-year-olds who are solitary but involved in constructive activities. They move away from interacting with others rather than toward them (Rubin, 2002). Professionals must pay attention to and not neglect social withdrawal and social isolation. Licensed psychologists can diagnose social anxiety disorder (SAD) as early as two years of age. These children exhibit marked and persistent fear of social situations (Buss et al., 2013; Gazelle, 2010). You may also see other signs of anxiety in children who feel socially fearful, such as thumb sucking, lip biting, and hair pulling. Other children actively refuse peer initiatives rather than avoid them (Williams et al., 2007). Both

children who are withdrawn and those who refuse peer advances may be fearful of others and new situations (Henderson, Marshall, Fox, and Rubin, 2004). Their heart rates increase when they watch other toddlers play. Unfortunately, infants, toddlers, and two-year-olds who are withdrawn and socially anxious are more likely to experience emotional and behavioral problems at three and five years (Guedeny et al., 2014). They more likely face peer rejection in their elementary years (Gazell, 2006).

Some children do not reject others; rather, their peers reject them. These toddlers and two-year-olds may wander around trying to join others' play. Rejection has detrimental effects on young children. Do toddlers and two-year-olds reject some of their peers? It seems that they do. We have observed peers continuously run away from a toddler in a program. Toddlers who use aggressive tactics are more likely to be rejected.

Children Who Feel Traumatized or Experience Child Abuse or Neglect

To an infant or toddler, trauma comes in many forms. A child may witness or experience violence at home or in the neighborhood. A child may experience separation from a loved one or may be the victim of child abuse or neglect.

Children who experience trauma are fearful. They feel unsettled and upset. They have lost the ability to predict what happens next. They may cry and not sleep well. They may cling tightly to favorite adults and become "human Velcro" (Schechter et al., 2002). Some infants and toddlers withdraw into a world of their own. Others will become aggressive because of their frightened and angry feelings. Young children who have been abused or neglected may suffer from chronic malnutrition, head injury resulting in brain damage, hearing loss, poor motor control, developmental delays, attachment disorders, lack of basic trust, "frozen watchfulness," anxiety, aggression, and language delays (Wiggins, Feneschel, and Mann, 2007). These results of abuse or neglect influence peer behavior as well as adult-child relationships. Children who feel traumatized cannot interact normally with their peers when they feel so worried about the safety of themselves and others.

Children whose family members experience trauma, such as a death in the family or a car accident, often lose their "insulation of affection" (Solnit, 2002) from their family. Joy Osofsky (2002) explains how infants, toddlers, and two-year-olds might react to traumatic events that affect their parents and other adults in their lives. She asserts that one-year-olds need reassurance from adults. They react to the tensions, stress, anxiety, and fear of the trusted adult and need an adult to hold them and hug them and tell them everything is going to be all right. A two-year-old will understand more that something terrible has happened, that people have been hurt, and that people are anxious and sad. Since children of this age tend to feel very powerful, they may even think they have done something to "cause" this awful thing to happen. They need adults to tell them details in simple language and to reassure them they are safe and protected.

In the third year, children will understand more but will have difficulty knowing the difference between pretend and real. Children are likely to repeat the traumatic event through play to try to master it. If they seem stuck in their play, for example acting out a car accident or an injury over and over, you may suggest a different more positive ending.

Children with Disabilities

Children with disabilities vary in their needs, strengths, and interests. Each child is an individual. For example, while most children with autism spectrum disorder experience social challenges, each child differs in his language, motor, and social skills. Use the strategies identified in each chapter of this book with children who have identified disabilities, to increase their social attitudes, opportunities, and skills as well as their communication skills and their inclusion in programs. Wonderful resources for enhancing the social skills of children with disabilities include the Center on the Social and Emotional Foundations for Early Learning (CSEFEL) and the Technical Assistance Center on Social Emotional Intervention for Young Children (TACSEI).

Final Thoughts

Reflect on Your Feelings

Reflecting on your feelings about children who feel challenged and the needs of the children is a great place to start before deciding on specific strategies to use. Documenting children's areas of challenge and strengths as well as the purpose of their behavior provides the information to individualize strategies.

Reflect on your feelings. We feel sad when babies feel tension, cope without continuity, and live without love. We struggle to make sense of the insensible: families without homes, children suddenly without parents, and abuse and neglect of vulnerable babies. Some adults may feel anger at the unfairness and inequity across the world. We admire babies, families, and their resilience and yet worry that, if risk factors accumulate, the chances for a child's healthy development and sense of well-being will be challenged. We often feel helpless to make a difference in the lives of young children and their families, and we often feel a sense of urgency because of our knowledge of the importance of the early years.

Reflect on the Needs of Children

While empathizing with the challenges that young children feel, note the coping strategies of children that may sometimes seem like challenges to adults. Admire the spirit of a child who cries in hopes that someone will come to soothe him. He has not given up. Respect the coping skills of a one-year-old who holds his hands up to a teacher to be held, even though the infant's previous teacher did not believe in holding him for fear of spoiling him. He has not given up. Admire the feistiness of a two-year-old who tries to get his needs met, even though many of those needs were not met in the past. This child has not given up. Try to put yourself in the minds and bodies of the children and determine what needs they have and the behaviors they have learned to get those needs met. Children have learned behaviors to cope with their environment that are challenging to adults and peers. We need to support children to find more relational ways of getting their needs met.

Kelly, Zuckerman, Sandoval, and Buehlman (2001) identified ten needs of infants and toddlers. If any of these needs are not met, then the young child may experience relationship challenges.

- To feel safe and secure
- To feel worthy and loved
- To have mutually enjoyable relationships and feel a sense of belonging
- To feel acknowledged and understood
- To feel noticed and receive attention
- To feel a sense of control and predictability
- To understand and manage upset feelings
- To feel safe and stimulated in my exploration
- To feel competent
- To be heard and communicate

Discuss these needs with team members and families. Ask how these needs are met at home and in the program, and who meets these needs. Discuss how a child might demonstrate that his needs are met or unmet. If a child has an unmet need, how can programs and families work together to ensure that the need is met?

Document Children's Strengths and Needs

Use charts like the following to document specific behaviors of older infants, toddlers, and two-year-olds to develop an intervention plan that considers their social challenges and builds on strengths. Observe a child for a period, such as fifteen minutes a day for five days. Tally how many times the child displays the listed behaviors. Then use the information to understand the child's strengths and challenges and to help the child express negative feelings appropriately and use sociable and prosocial behavior.

From Biting to Hugging: Understanding Social Development in Infants and Toddlers

Name:_____

Behavior	Date/Time
• Sociable:	
» Shows interest in peers	_____
» Smiles at peers	_____
» Initiates play with peers	_____
» Responds to peers' attempts to initiate play by joining them	_____
» Imitates the actions or expressions of peers	_____
» Is involved in rituals, games, and reciprocal interactions	_____
» Has a friend	_____
• Prosocial:	
» Shows empathy	_____
» Helps other children	_____
» Comforts other children in distress	_____
• Active refusal and rejection of peers:	
» Refuses peers' attempts to play	_____
» Turns his or her back toward or moves away from peers	_____
• Withdraws from peers:	
» Watches rather than participates	_____
» Acts as if he or she does not notice peers' attempts to initiate play	_____
» Cries or fusses easily around peers	_____
• Is rejected by peers:	
» Peers push him or her away or reject physically	_____
» Peers ignore him or her	_____
• Is negative or aggressive with peers:	
» Hits, pushes, or in other ways hurts other children	_____
» Takes toys or other objects from peers with force	_____
» Scares peers with noises, faces, or other actions	_____

Source: Adaptation of Williams, Ontai, and Mastergeorge (2007) observation instrument.

Document the Purpose of Children's Behavior

When you identify a challenging behavior, observe and document what, when, where, and how a child behaves to figure out why a child might use aggression or show anger, hit, bite, withdraw, reject peers, or be rejected. Through using a chart like the following, teachers and families can begin to understand what the child might be trying to accomplish with the behavior. In this example, the teachers are trying to understand two-year-old Kenneth's biting.

Name: Kenneth

What happened prior to the behavior?	Behavior	What happened after the behavior?
Sienna pushed Kenneth.	Kenneth bit Sienna on the arm.	Sienna cried, and Miss Shelley came to intervene.
Tommy reached in front of Kenneth to get a toy on the shelf.	Kenneth bit Tommy on the arm.	Tommy yelled, and Ms. Latoya came to intervene.
Matti tried to sit near Kenneth, who was on the floor looking at a book.	Kenneth bit Matti on her shoulder.	Matti cried, and Ms. Latoya came to intervene.

From these observations, the teachers thought about what they wished Kenneth would do in these situations. They hoped that he would learn to "use his words" but knew that he was not quite ready to do that. They taught him how to use the sign *stop* when other children came too close to him. They practiced it with him many times during the day. At other times, the teachers focused on encouraging Kenneth to comfort other children in distress and play near one other child with a teacher nearby. The teachers gave Kenneth attention by using encouraging and affirming words with him. They held him when he needed to be held and gave him additional positive attention throughout the day. Soon Kenneth used sign language and seemed to enjoy his peers being near.

Support Families

Children's secure attachments to family members and teachers are necessary for children to thrive. Strategies used with a child who feels challenged with peers are more likely to be successful when teachers create a relationship plan with family members. For children with intense, ongoing, and serious challenges, mental-health services support everyone involved.

We want to support families so that they create secure attachments with their children. In all the chapters in this book we have emphasized the positive effects of children feeling secure with their familiar adults. In addition, secure attachment reduces the negative effects of stress on young children (Gunnar and Sullivan, 2017). Feeling secure with all of children's familiar caregivers is ideal; however, even one secure attachment has benefits for a child. Feeling uncertain, anxious, or avoidant with both parents contributes to a child's risk for behavioral challenges (Kochanska and Kim, 2013).

Develop a relationship plan for the child with families and team members. Ask, "Who has the meaningful relationships with this child? How can those with meaningful relationships with the child:

- help the child feel safe?

- meet all his or her emotional needs?

- provide nurturing routines?

- provide continuity of care?

- develop trust that he or she will grow each day with sensitive responsive care?

- support the child's development of a positive working model of relationships?

- build on the child's strengths to support prosocial attitudes and behaviors?

Mental-health services support relationships for children who feel challenged as well as for families and teachers who are challenged by children. Professionals in collaboration with families, teachers, and community members typically provide the services.

• • •

Some young children experience peer relationship challenges due to their temperament, relationship experiences, or the settings that they encounter daily at home or in a program. Adults feel challenged by these children, while the children feel challenged by the adults and their environment. When children bite others, children, teachers, and parents are concerned.

Strategies tailored to the needs and motivations of the children work best. When children suffer from grief, trauma, aggression, abuse, or neglect, their sad, angry, or helpless feelings spill over to their peers. They may withdraw or lash out angrily on certain days or every day. Astute teachers understand the emotional and social needs of young children and attempt to meet those needs. Teachers create caring communities where infants and toddlers receive finely tuned, sensitive, and enjoyable interactions with a focus on satisfying adult-child and peer relationships.

Chapter
NINE

Strategies for Supporting Children Who Feel
Challenged by Peer Relationships

When children's behavior is challenging to adults, we must remember that the children themselves are feeling challenged and frustrated. There are many strategies that meet the emotional and relationship needs of young children and guide them to learn more effective ways of getting their needs met. What follows is a summary of the strategies to use when children are feeling challenged with peer relationships.

Strategies for Biting that Make a Difference

Reflect, Observe, and Document

Children bite for a variety of reasons. A child may be struggling with the ideas of holding on and letting go. She may be learning the concept of autonomy, exploring, or learning about cause and effect. The child may be teething. She may be attempting to interact with peers or imitating behavior she has seen. She may be stressed, anxious, angry, or frustrated. She may be trying to get attention. To successfully address the biting, observe the reason or goal of the behavior, and then try some of the following strategies to help the child learn more acceptable, prosocial ways to meet that goal.

Reason for Biting: Holding On and Letting Go

- Help ease infant and toddler separations from their family members at the beginning of the day.

- Give children practice with holding on and letting go of toys or other desired objects by offering opportunities such as putting blocks into containers.

- Do not pressure toilet learning. Wait until the child shows that she can "let go" in other areas of life.

Reason for Biting: Autonomy

- Provide as many opportunities as possible for children to choose and have power. For example, offer a choice between a red marker and a blue marker, the Cheerios or the Rice Krispies, or milk or no milk on their cereal.

- Give children long stretches of time to choose, explore, and learn.

- Provide safe guidance boundaries for them. Without limits, children can actually feel more out of control.

Reason for Biting: Exploration

- Provide a variety of sensory-motor experiences in the centers.

- Ensure opportunities for the infants and toddlers to practice blossoming motor skills. Provide private spaces where a child can concentrate on a task such as putting together a puzzle without peer intrusion.

Reason for Biting: Teething

- Provide the infant or toddler with safe teething toys.

- Older children can be encouraged to bite on foods and firm teething toys.

- Keep clean frozen cloths on hand to provide cooling relief for the teething toddler and for the child who has been bitten.

Reason for Biting: Desire for Peer Interaction

- Children need lots of social experiences to learn how to interact with others.

- Teach children how to be gentle.

- Acknowledge a child's interest in other children by saying, "I know you like Darin. You can give him a toy."

- Notice and acknowledge positive peer interaction such as one child hugging another, giving a toy to another, and smiling to another.

Reason for Biting: Cause and Effect

- Provide toys that do something—make a noise, move, light up—when the child acts on them.

- Provide sand, dirt, water, paints, blocks, and crayons that support creative, open-ended sensory experiences. Offer many opportunities for the child to use materials to make something happen.

- Help children notice the positive reaction they get when they pat, hug, or give a toy to another child.

Reason for Biting: Imitation

- Model loving, nurturing, sharing, polite, positive behavior for young children to imitate.

- Develop a repertoire of behaviors for handling children's hurtful behavior that models relationship-restoration strategies.

- Model talking about feelings.

- Use positive techniques that emphasize the perspectives of others for children to imitate.

- Support children using their words or sign language to prevent biting and to restore relationships.

Reason for Biting: Attention

- At times when no biting occurs, nurture the child who bites with positive, warm attention.

- Notice, comment on, and support children's positive, busy, curious, helpful, productive behaviors.

- Break the negative cycle of child behavior with adult positive comments and hugs for desirable behavior.

Reasons for Biting: Frustration

- Acknowledge the feelings of children. "Mark has the truck right now. You are feeling frustrated about having to wait."

- Teach children language, such as, "I feel frustrated."

- Examine your environment:
  - » Are there too many children?
  - » Are there cozy corners?
  - » Is the environment cluttered?

Reason for Biting: Anger

- Meet the child's needs for loving care.

- Build trust with a child by being consistently responsive.

- Say, "I do not want you to hit. I can help you."

- Help the young child to develop a repertoire of behaviors for handling angry feelings.

- Help the child to learn how to say or use sign language to communicate *no* to another child who grabs a toy.

Reason for Biting: Stress and Anxiety

- Work with parents to determine the source of a child's stress.

- With the child, provide calming activities such as water or sand play.

- Allow the child to suck a thumb or hold a transitional object such as a blanket or stuffed animal.

- Provide one-on-one time with a special adult.

- Rock, pat backs, and sing songs at nap time to quiet children into sleep. Play soothing lullabies.

- Stay close to nurture the child and help the child through transition times.

- Talk soothingly to the child about the things going on in her life.

- Caring adults will need to help these children connect with their own emotions as well as others' emotions.

Use Adult-Child Relationship-Based Strategies

The moment when a child bites another child can be stressful and upsetting for everybody involved. Take a deep breath, and remember that this is an opportunity for teaching. If punishment for the child who bit is harsh, the young child may nurse her own hurt rather than concentrating on helping the victim of the bite. Help children learn positive strategies instead of biting. Do not use punishment, name calling, shaming, or love withdrawal.

- Support both children emotionally.

- Teach different strategies to children.

- Use techniques that restore relationships.

- Ask what happened, or state the problem. As you talk with the children, remember to use words and/ or actions that are appropriate to the children's developmental level.

- Ask about or emphasize the perspective and feelings of the child who was hurt.

- Do not discount the biter as a person with feelings, too.

- Ask or state an alternative approach.

- Encourage the child who bit to think of how to help the other child feel better.

- Follow the protocol for your program.

Observe when the biting occurs. Keep records and look for patterns—does the biting typically occur in a crowded center? Is the child biting after a parent drops her off?

If one child's biting continues after several days of repeating these techniques, meet with the family and other teachers to figure out what might be causing the child to bite. Plan with the family to determine consistent approaches across home and the learning program. Problem solve strategies, and then review the results with the family and the teaching team. If one strategy does not work, try another approach.

Use a system of "time-in." Have an adult shadow the child, meet the child's emotional needs, show the child affection and encouragement, and catch her before she bites. This adult can teach her alternative behaviors and can help her learn how to be gentle or use sign language or words to express her needs.

Be proactive with staff. In a staff meeting, review all the reasons that young children bite and all the techniques that teachers can use. All programs need to create a protocol for handling biting incidents. Individualize strategies for a child and then work together as a team to provide caring relationships and consistency for that child.

Be proactive with parents and families. Before parents become upset about a biting problem, hold a parent meeting or send a newsletter home to let parents know about the relationship-restoration techniques they and the staff can use. Parents need to know why young children bite, that it is a common problem whenever young children are together in a group, and that the staff do everything possible to ensure the safety of the children. Send home a handout on why biting happens and include the strategies that you use to help children who bite and the children who receive the bites. Explain the protocol your center follows when biting occurs. Many programs have decided that they will not reveal the name of the child who bit. What is your program's protocol?

Strategies for Anger, Defiance, and Aggressive Behaviors that Make a Difference

Children's behavior is an attempt to communicate. When a child expresses anger or defiance or acts aggressively, consider what may be driving this behavior.

Reflect, Observe, and Document

- Consider the health of the child. Consider sleep needs and possible iron deficiency or lead poisoning.

- Assess children's hearing and language development.

- Observe children's anger behavior carefully to figure out what and who makes them angry and how they express their anger.

- Reflect on when children are defiant and how they express defiance. Are their defiant behaviors accompanied by aggressive behaviors?

- Reflect on children's temperament needs. Children with exuberant temperaments may need help with self-regulation. Children with irritable temperaments may need to be introduced to a few peers at a time.

- Observe and reflect with the team and the family of a child who uses hurtful behaviors. Ask who the child is aggressive with—parents, teachers, peers?

- What types of aggression does the child use?

- Is the child experiencing toxic stress?

- What are the goals that the child tries to achieve with aggression?

- What are the emotional needs of the child? Are the needs being met?

- Do hitting or other aggressive acts help the child regulate strong emotions and feel in control again?

- Has the child learned that aggression is a way to get an adult or a peer to pay attention to her?

- Is the child imitating adults in his life? Alternatively, does the child not know other ways to solve problems?

Use Adult-Child Relationship-Based Strategies

When you have observed, reflected, and learned more about what the children's behaviors are and when and why the behaviors are occurring, try the following strategies to help the children learn new ways to meet their needs.

- Show empathy and warmth, and be responsive. These children are often frightened by their inability to control strong emotions. Children who are highly angry benefit from high maternal warmth (Razza et al., 2012).

- Build trust by spending time alone with infants and toddlers. Allow infants to drape on your body, and allow toddlers to stay by your side if they'd like. Once they feel secure, they will be off exploring again. Welcome them back when they need to return to you to receive emotional comfort and strength to venture off again.

- Establish reciprocal (equal) turn-taking chains of communication with children to help them engage, learn turn-taking skills, feel acknowledged, and learn to listen.

- Follow children's lead during play to help them feel effective and motivated to continue play. Adult intrusion and coercion may lead to children's angry, defiant, and aggressive behavior.

- Pair a child who feels angry or aggressive with one who is generally sociable. Stay with them to support peer interactions.

- Acknowledge feelings constantly—actively listen with your eyes and ears to what the child is feeling. Say, "You seem to feel sad. What can I do to help?" Or, "That made you so mad." Or "It seems like you got so frustrated. Your hands did something you didn't want them to do. I know that doesn't feel good."

- Teach children feeling and emotion words to use. Children have the right to feel strong emotions. They have the right to use words to express their feelings and to have the freedom to say them. They have the right to be heard.

- Work on children's perspective-taking with peers. Help them "read" the emotions of others.

- Give reasons why certain behaviors are expected. State and restate rules for how we treat each other well. Say, "We are gentle with our friends. Friends like that."

- Teach, teach, teach alternative behaviors to aggression with peers.

- Reduce stress in the children's lives both at home and in the program. Allow children to stay near you when they need additional emotional support. In some centers, certain days when an infant or toddler needs abundant emotional support are called "Care of the Spirit" days (Colorado EQ Project, 2017).

- Engage children in prosocial activities. Bring them along to help children who are distressed.

- Create social stories using the child's name. Tell the story from the child's perspective. Identify and explain strategies that "Kayla" used when she was so angry she felt like stomping her feet. Create a piece of the story in which Kayla makes a friend by helping her peer.

- Intervene immediately when a child's anger builds and give children a choice of strategies to use—using their words; going to the teacher; stomping; going limp; throwing a ball into a basket; or going to a cozy corner with soft blankets, stuffed animals, and dolls. Limit the choices to two for toddlers. Add more when children can process more than two choices.

- Stop children who become aggressive. They need someone to provide clear boundaries for their behavior. Give choices to encourage self-regulation. Say, for example, "You feel very angry. Can you stop throwing chairs or do you need me to stop you?" "I see you need me to stop you. I will hold you to help you."

- Show you care about the child by preventing and stopping risky behavior. Children who engage in risky behavior may be looking for someone to care enough to stop them (Koplow, 1996; Lieberman, 1993).

- Give ten times more attention to children for sociable behaviors than for aggressive behaviors.

- Express that you still care for and love them even when they behave angrily, defiantly, or aggressively.

Create a Caring Community—Environment and Responsive Program Planning

Create a caring community in your classroom and in your center. Engage families by encouraging visits to the program.

- Provide an interesting environment, and give the children time to choose and focus on activities that interest them.

- Provide activities that soothe children, such as sand play, water play, and painting. These activities calm children and help them learn to focus. Give children their own bins of sand or water, but place the bins close enough so that children can watch and talk to each other.

- Provide cozy corners where one or two children can play together without a throng of children. Sometimes children who feel aggressive do not like to be crowded by peers.

- Provide a cozy corner for one child, such as a box, a small (empty) play pool with a blanket, or a cubby, where children can go when they are feeling frustrated. This is not a time-out area. It is child-chosen time-in where a little one can relax and become self-regulated.

- Do not herd children around together. This increases children's stress levels and increases the likelihood of conflict and aggression.

Support Families

Discuss with family members what they think may be causing their child to feel angry, aggressive, or defiant. Problem solve with families for solutions at home and in the program. Share the strategies that work in the program with families, and ask parents if they think they would work at home. Try the solutions and then review with families how they worked.

Provide emotional support, social support, and information to prevent and ameliorate harsh parenting practices and promote secure attachments. In one research study, parents who were given very brief research summaries concerning how corporal punishment relates to children's behavioral challenges changed their attitudes about spanking (Holden et al., 2014).

If children's opposition, anger, and aggressive behaviors are severe and continuous, then work with community agencies to provide mental-health services to support the children, classroom teachers, and the children's families.

From Biting to Hugging: Understanding Social Development in Infants and Toddlers

Strategies for Children Who Feel Shy, Cautious, Anxious, Inhibited, Withdrawn, Rejected, or Fearful

Reflect, Observe, and Document

- Consider cultural factors. Rubin (1998), in his examination of social and emotional development from a cultural perspective, emphasized that the mothers he interviewed in China did not view shyness and inhibition as negative traits. Another study concluded that Chinese parents, however, do not want their children to be withdrawn (Cheah et al., 2004).

- Consider temperament. There may be a temperamental factor at play. Some children are more reticent to enter play. They need to know exactly what is happening before they step into a situation. Other children may be sensitive to touch and not want to sit close to other children or join a crowd. Loud noises may bother others, so these children try to find a quiet corner in the room.

- Observe for hearing challenges and delayed language skills that may contribute to children's withdrawn behavior.

- Consider the fear factor. There may be a fear factor to withdrawing or actively refusing peers. Teachers can observe the child and talk with family members to determine the source and content of a child's fears.

Use Adult-Child Relationship-Based Strategies

Develop a strong, positive relationship with the child, as trust in the adult is a necessary ingredient for infants and toddlers to feel socially safe. Help infants and toddlers feel safe by responding to their physical and emotional needs. Greet every child warmly in the morning, helping each child feel your affectionate regard. After trust is developed with a teacher, then a teacher can bring a peer along to greet a child.

Inform children of all ages what will happen next during the day. This helps alleviate anxiety. Be available for holding and hugs when a child shows fear. When adults do not respond to children for fear of spoiling them, a child's independence is not increased. In fact, when teachers reject children, the children may become more dependent or more withdrawn as their fears for their own safety grow.

Scaffold social success for the child who is withdrawn. If an infant or toddler clings to adults in a program, slowly introduce the child to materials and activities. Hold an infant who seems fearful of peers while gradually introducing her to peers. Stay with a toddler to help her enter an outdoor sandbox with peers. Remain nearby and help the child get started with play. Use encouraging words and be patient. Set up opportunities for two children inside with a teacher while others go outside with other teachers.

Overprotectiveness can contribute to children feeling fearful. Research has shown that protective caregiver behavior may contribute to toddler distress in new situations (Hutt et al., 2013). Provide safe risk opportunities tailored to the individual child. Scaffold children's successes with activities that seem somewhat risky to the young child. For example, a small slide may provide a challenge to a child who is fearful. With your support, the child will feel competent after tackling her fear of the slide.

Teach prosocial behaviors to the children who are rejected rather than just eliminate behaviors that contribute to others' rejection of them (Hay, 2006). This is crucially important! Scaffold social success for the child who is rejected. Provide the child many opportunities for success with adults, toys, and materials. Build the child's sense of self-worth. Comment to others when the child does something interesting. Give the child a new toy, and ask the child to show other toddlers and two-year-olds how it works.

Create a Caring Community

Create a comfort corner where children may go when they feel sad or want to be alone.

Provide another cozy corner with enough room for a child and a friend or teacher. Place soft animals, a quilt, and books in the comfort corners to soothe children.

Provide primary care. Whenever possible, assign a teacher to the same small group of children to provide diapering, feeding, rocking, and patting to sleep. This helps a child develop trust in familiar adults and alleviates fears.

Support Families

Inhibited toddlers may be challenging for parents who want their children to be socially competent. Parents may believe that controlling or chiding toddlers encourages them to interact with their peers. However, patience, support, and a gradual introduction of these toddlers to peers result in better social outcomes (Kiel et al., 2016). Support parents to provide safe risk opportunities for children with fears.

Discuss the behavior with the child's family. Perhaps, the family's goal is to create a child who is quiet and respectful of others. However, the parents may not want their child to withdraw or actively avoid other children. Listen to the family's perspective and work collaboratively with them to support the child's social competence in a way that is culturally relevant. Encourage families to create playdates with children who are younger to give the child who is rejected or withdrawn opportunities for social success.

From Biting to Hugging: Understanding Social Development in Infants and Toddlers

Strategies with Children Who Have Experienced Trauma, Abuse, or Neglect

Reflect, Observe, and Document

- As always, first ensure that children receive a comprehensive health check, including hearing.

- Understand that children may regress in their development. Older infants who loved to explore may want to be on a teacher's lap most of the day. Toddlers who were eating with a spoon may eat with their fingers. Two-year-olds who were learning to use a toilet may have accidents and want their diapers back. Children who separated easily from their families at the beginning of the day may cry and scream when a parent must leave.

- Document behaviors that may indicate trauma, including child abuse and neglect. Keep reports of any unusual marks or wounds on a child. Document children's dazed, aggressive, or withdrawn behavior.

Use Adult-Child Relationship-Based Strategies

- Most important, have empathy for the child's experience. Ask, "What must this be like for this child?" and "Can this child predict what will happen in her life?"

- Provide protection and affection for children experiencing trauma. Use physical touch in responsive ways. Some children may not let you hug them; however, they might sit next to you. Let them know that they are safe with you and in your program. Use soothing and comforting words. Be an emotional haven for them and their families. Be patient, gentle, and loving.

- Provide boundaries for children who test adults to see if the adults care enough to stop their dangerous behavior. Say, "I do not want you to climb on the bookshelf. The bookshelf can fall over. I keep you safe here."

- Children who have experienced trauma may feel angry and aggressive toward adults and peers. They need the opposite from adults, not more aggression and anger, which continues a cycle of negative interactions.

Create a Caring Community

- Use strategies that create a predictable environment. For example, if a child likes to paint, then provide paint every day so the child can count on the opportunity being there when she needs it.

- Provide consistent routines. For example, after lunch, have toddlers and two-year-olds wash their hands, pick out a book, and go to their cots, where they find their blankets and lovies waiting for them. A teacher can then sit between two children and pat them on their backs (if this is what comforts them) while singing softly to them.

- Create a corner in the room where one toddler can be alone with a teacher or two toddlers can be together.

- Encourage play with art materials, sand, and water. However, give the child experiencing trauma her own materials, bin of sand or water, and space. Place the child close to others.

Support Families

- Constantly exchange information with families. Dialog with families if the program and families have conflicting beliefs.

- Work closely with foster or adoptive parents of children who have been abused to help them understand the effects of trauma on a child and strategies to use.

- Work collaboratively with community mental-health services for assessments and intervention

- Provide continuity of care in which a child's beloved and trusted teacher moves with the child (and a group of peers) to a new room as the child grows. Work to keep secure adult-child and peer attachment relationships intact.

strategies with the children, their families, and program staff.

- Final strategies for children who feel challenged with peer relationships:
  » Reflect on your feelings
  » Reflect on the needs of children
  » Document children's strength and needs
  » Document the purpose of children's behavior
  » Support families

Summary of Strategies

The following are some strategies to try with children who feel angry, defiant, and/or use aggressive behaviors.

- Reflect, observe, and document:
  » Consider the health of the children. Consider sleep needs and possible iron deficiency or lead poisoning.

  » Assess children's hearing and language development.

  » Observe children's anger behavior carefully to figure out what and who makes them angry and how they express their anger.

  » Reflect on when children are defiant and how they express defiance. Are their defiant behaviors accompanied by aggressive behaviors?

  » Reflect on children's temperament needs. Children with exuberant temperaments may need help with self-regulation. Children with irritable temperaments may need to be introduced to a few peers at a time.

  » Observe and reflect with the team and the family of a child who uses hurtful behaviors. Ask who the child is aggressive with—parents, teachers, and/or peers? What types of aggression does the child use? Is the child experiencing toxic stress? What are the goals that the child tries to achieve with aggression? What are the emotional needs of the child? Are the needs being met? Do hitting or other aggressive acts help the child regulate strong emotions and feel in control again? Has the child learned that aggression is a way to get an adult or peer to pay attention to her? Is the child imitating adults in her life? Alternatively, does the child not know other ways to solve problems?

- Use adult-child relationship-based strategies:

  » Show empathy and warmth, and be responsive to meet children's needs. These children are often frightened by their inability to control strong emotions. Children who are highly angry benefit from high maternal warmth (Razza et al., 2012).

  » Build trust by spending time alone with infants and toddlers. Allow infants to drape on your body, and allow toddlers to stay by your side if they'd like. Once they feel secure, they will be off exploring again. Welcome them back when they need to return to you to receive emotional comfort and strength to venture off again.

  » Establish reciprocal turn-taking chains of communication with children to help them engage, learn turn-taking skills, feel acknowledged, and learn to listen.

  » Follow children's lead during play to help them feel effective and motivated to continue play. Adult intrusion and coercion may lead to children's angry, defiant, and aggressive behavior.

  » Pair a child who feels angry or aggressive with one who is generally sociable. Stay with them to support peer interactions.

  » Acknowledge feelings constantly—actively listen with your eyes and ears to what the child is feeling. Say, "You seem to feel sad. What can I do to help?" Or, "That made you so mad." Or "It seems like you got so frustrated. Your hands did something you didn't want them to do. I know that doesn't feel good."

  » Teach children feeling and emotion words to use. Children have the right to feel strong emotions. They have the right to use words to express their feelings and to have the freedom to say them. They have the right to be heard.

» Work on children's perspective taking with peers. Help them "read" the emotions of others.

» Give reasons why certain behaviors are expected. State and restate rules for how we treat each other well. Say, "We are gentle with our friends. Friends like that."

» Teach, teach, teach alternative behaviors to aggression with peers.

» Reduce stress in the children's lives both at home and in the program. Allow children to stay near you when they need additional emotional support. In some centers, certain days when an infant or toddler needs abundant emotional support is called "Care of the Spirit" day (Colorado EQ Project, 2017).

» Engage children in prosocial activities. Bring them along to help children who are distressed.

» Create social stories using the child's name. Tell the story from the child's perspective. Identify and explain strategies that "Kayla" used when she was so angry she felt like stomping her feet. Create a piece of the story where Kayla makes a friend by helping her peer.

» Intervene immediately when a child's anger builds, and give children a choice of strategies to use—using their words; going to the teacher; stomping; going limp; throwing a ball into a basket; or going to a cozy corner with soft blankets, stuffed animals, and dolls. Limit the choices to two for toddlers. Add more when children can process more than two choices.

» Stop children who become aggressive. They need someone to provide clear boundaries for their behavior. Give choices to encourage self-regulation. Say, for example, "You feel very angry. Can you stop throwing chairs or do you need me to stop you?" "I see you need me to stop you. I will hold you to help you."

» Show you care about the child by preventing and stopping risky behavior. Children who engage in risky behavior may be looking for someone to care enough to stop them (Koplow, 1996; Lieberman, 1993).

» Give ten times more attention to children for sociable behaviors than for aggressive behaviors.

» Express that you still care for and love them even when they behave angrily, defiantly, or aggressively.

• Create a caring community:

» Provide an interesting environment with time for children to choose and focus on activities that interest them.

» Do not herd children around together. This increases children's stress levels and increases the likelihood of conflict and aggression.

» Provide cozy corners where one or two children can play together without a throng of children. Sometimes children who feel aggressive do not like to be crowded by peers.

» Provide a cozy corner for one child, such as a box, a small (empty) play pool with a blanket, or a cubby, for children to go to when they are feeling frustrated. This is not a time-out area. It is child-chosen time-in to relax and become self-regulated.

» Provide activities that soothe children, such as sand play, water play, and painting. These activities calm children and help them learn to focus to learn. Give children their own bins of sand or water, but place the bins close enough so that children can watch and talk to each other.

• Support families:

» Discuss with families what they think may be causing the children to feel angry, aggressive, or defiant. Problem solve with families for solutions at home and in the program. Try the solutions and then review with families how they worked.

» Share the strategies that work in the program with families. Ask parents if they think they would work at home.

» Provide emotional support, social support, and information to prevent and ameliorate harsh parenting practices and promote secure attachments. In one research study, parents who were given very brief research summaries concerning how corporal punishment relates to children's behavioral challenges changed their attitudes about spanking (Holden et al., 2014).

» Engage families by encouraging visits to the program.

» If children's opposition, anger, and aggressive behaviors are severe and continuous, then work with community agencies to provide mental-health services to support the children, classroom teachers, and the children's families.

Summary of Strategies

The following are strategies that adults can use to help children who feel shy, cautious, anxious, inhibited, withdrawn, rejected, or fearful.

• Reflect, observe, and document:

» Consider cultural factors. Rubin (1998) in his examination of social and emotional development from a cultural perspective emphasized that the mothers he interviewed in China did not view shyness and inhibition as negative traits. Another study concluded that Chinese parents, however, do not want their children to be withdrawn (Cheah et al., 2004).

» Consider temperament. There may be a temperamental factor at play. Some children are more reticent to enter play. They need to know exactly what is happening before they step into a situation. Other children may be sensitive to touch and not want to sit close to other children or join a crowd. Loud noises may bother others, so these children try to find a quiet corner in the room.

» Observe for hearing challenges and delayed language skills that may contribute to children's withdrawn behavior.

» Consider the fear factor. There may be a fear factor to withdrawing or actively refusing peers. Teachers can observe the child and talk with family members to determine the source and content of a child's fears.

- Use adult-child relationship-based strategies:
  - » Develop a strong, positive relationship with the child, as trust in the adult is a necessary ingredient for infants and toddlers to feel socially safe. Help infants and toddlers feel safe by responding to their physical and emotional needs.
  - » Greet every child warmly in the morning, helping each child feel your affectionate regard. After trust is developed with a teacher, then a teacher can bring a peer along to greet a child.
  - » Inform children of all ages what will happen next during the day. This helps alleviate their anxiety.
  - » Be available for holding and hugs when a child shows fear. When adults do not respond to children for fear of "spoiling" them, a child's independence is not increased. In fact, when teachers reject children, the children may become more dependent or more withdrawn as their fears for their own safety grow.
  - » Scaffold social success for the child who is withdrawn. If an infant or toddler clings to adults in a program, slowly introduce the child to materials and activities. Hold an infant who seems fearful of peers while gradually introducing him to peers. Stay with a toddler to enter an outdoor sandbox with peers. Stay near and help the child get started with play. Use encouraging words and be patient.
  - » Set up opportunities for two children inside with a teacher while others go outside with other teachers.
  - » Overprotectiveness can contribute to children feeling fearful. Research has shown that caregiver protective behavior may contribute to toddler distress in new situations (Hutt et al., 2013). Provide safe risk opportunities tailored to the individual child. Scaffold children's successes with activities that seem somewhat risky to the young child. For example, a small slide may provide a challenge to a child who is fearful. With your support, the child will feel competent after tackling her fear of the slide.
  - » Teach prosocial behaviors to the children who are rejected rather than just eliminate behaviors that contribute to others' rejection of them (Hay, 2006). This is crucially important!
  - » Scaffold social success for the child who is rejected. Provide the child many opportunities for success with adults, toys, and materials. Build the child's sense of self-worth. Comment to others when the child does something interesting. Give the child a new toy, and ask the child to show other toddlers and two-year-olds how it works.
- Create a caring community:
  - » Create a comfort corner where children may go when they feel sad or want to be alone. Provide another cozy corner with enough room for a child and a friend or teacher. Place soft animals, a quilt, and books in the comfort corners to soothe children.
  - » Provide primary care. Whenever possible, assign a teacher to the same small group of children to provide diapering, feeding, rocking, and patting to sleep. This helps a child develop trust in familiar adults and alleviates fears.
- Support families:
  - » Inhibited toddlers may be challenging for parents who want their children to be socially competent. Parents may believe that controlling or chiding toddlers encourages them to interact with their peers. However, patience, support, and a gradual introduction of these toddlers to peers result in better social outcomes (Kiel et al., 2016).
  - » Support parents to provide safe risk opportunities for children with fears.

» Discuss the behavior with the child's family. Perhaps, the family's goal is to create a child who is quiet and respectful of others. However, the parents may not want their child to withdraw or actively avoid other children. Listen to the family's perspective and work collaboratively with them to support the child's social competence in a way that is culturally relevant.

» Encourage families to create playdates with children who are younger to give the child who is rejected or withdrawn opportunities for social success.

Summary of Strategies for Children Who Have Experienced Trauma, Abuse, or Neglect

- Reflect, observe, and document:

  » As always, first ensure that children receive a comprehensive health check, including hearing.

  » Understand that children may regress in their development. Older infants who loved to explore may want to be on a teacher's lap most of the day. Toddlers who were eating with a spoon may eat with their fingers. Two-year-olds who were learning to use a toilet may have accidents and want their diapers back. Children who separated easily from their families at the beginning of the day may cry and scream when a parent must leave.

  » Document behaviors that may indicate trauma, including child abuse and neglect. Keep reports of any unusual marks or wounds on a child. Document children's dazed, aggressive, or withdrawn behavior.

  » All states require that if certain defined persons know or **suspect** that child abuse is going on, the abuse must be reported to the authorities. These **mandatory reporting** laws were instituted to help promote awareness of child abuse and early intervention, if possible. Adults who work with young children are required to report.

- Use adult-child relationship-based strategies:

  » Most important, have empathy for the child's experience. Ask, "What must this be like for this child?" and "Can this child predict what will happen in her life?"

  » Provide protection and affection for children experiencing trauma. Use physical touch in responsive ways. Some children may not let you hug them; however, they might sit next to you. Let them know that they are safe with you and in your program. Use soothing and comforting words. Be an emotional haven for them and their families. Be patient, gentle, and loving.

  » Provide boundaries for children who test adults to see if the adults care enough to stop their dangerous behavior. Say, "I do not want you to climb on the bookshelf. The bookshelf can fall over. I keep you safe here."

  » Children who have experienced trauma may feel angry and aggressive toward adults and peers. They need the opposite from adults, not more aggression and anger that continues a cycle of negative interactions.

- Create a caring community:

  » Use strategies that create a predictable environment. For example, if a child likes to paint, then provide paint every day so the child can count on the opportunity being there when she needs it.

  » Provide consistent routines. For example, after lunch, have toddlers and two-year-olds wash their hands, pick out a book, and go to their cots, where they find their blankets and lovies waiting for them. A teacher can then sit between two children and pat them on their backs (if this is what comforts them) while singing softly to them.

  » Create a corner in the room where one toddler can be alone with a teacher or two toddlers can be together.

  » Encourage play with art materials, sand, and water. However, give the child experiencing trauma her own materials, bin of sand or water, and space. Place the child close to others.

  » Provide continuity of care in which a child's beloved and trusted teacher moves with the child (and a group of peers) to a new room as the child grows. Work to keep secure adult-child and peer attachment relationships intact.

- Support families:

  » Constantly exchange information with families. Dialogue with families if the program and families have conflicting beliefs.

  » Work closely with foster or adoptive parents of children who have been abused to help them understand the effects of trauma on a child and strategies to use.

  » Work collaboratively with community mental-health services for assessments and intervention strategies with the children, their families, and program staff.

  » Provide a resource library for families. The library could include the following materials:

Perry, Bruce, and Jana Rosenfelt. 2013. *A Child's Loss. Helping Children Exposed to Traumatic Death.* Houston, TX: Child Trauma Academy Press.

Resources from Child Welfare Information Gateway https://www.childwelfare.gov/topics/responding/trauma/caregivers/

Rice, Kathleen, and Betsy Groves. 2005. *Hope and Healing: A Caregiver's Guide to Helping Young Children Affected by Trauma.* Washington, DC: Zero to Three.

Appendix:

Complete Peer Behavior (Birth to Three)

0–4 Months

- Infants like to look at each other.

- By three to four months, an infant will smile at another infant.

- A three-month-old infant lying on his back will reach out to touch a peer next to him.

4–8 Months

- Infants like to look at, approach other infants, and initiate interaction (Selby and Bradley, 2003).

- Infants coo, smile, and laugh at each other (Porter, 2003).

- At five months, infants can match the vocal expressions (positive or negative) with the correct facial expressions of other infants (with two expressions shown side by side on a video). Infants gaze longer at the correct facial expression that matches the voice (Vaillant-Molina, Bahrick, and Flom, 2013).

- Infants as young as six months of age show more interest in peer strangers than adult strangers (Brooks and Lewis, 1976).

- Six-month-olds show more excitement at photos of six-month-olds than at photos of nine- and twelve-month-olds (Sanefuji, Ohgami, and Hashiya, 2006).

- Five- and ten-month-olds can make social judgments by choosing a helper puppet over one that was antisocial (Hamlin and Wynn, 2011).

- Six- and ten-month-old infants consider an individual's actions toward others in evaluating that individual as appealing or aversive; infants prefer an individual who helps another to one who hinders another, prefer a helping individual to a neutral individual, and prefer a neutral individual to a hindering individual. These findings constitute evidence that preverbal infants assess individuals based on their behavior toward others (Hamlin, Wynn, and Bloom, 2007).

- Infants may interact with peers with their whole body: rolling into them, crawling over them, licking or sucking on them, or sitting on them.

- Seven-month-olds discriminate between angry and fearful facial expressions and respond more to angry facial expressions (Kobiella, Grossmann, Reid, and Striano, 2008).

- Precursors to aggression can be seen in children at six months of age (Hay et al., 2014).

8–12 Months

- Infants like to touch each other and crawl around and beside each other.

- Infants may laugh gleefully at each other.

- Nine-month-olds prefer to look at photos and movies of babies their own age (Sanefuji, Ohgami, and Hashiya, 2006).

- Ten- to twelve-month-olds prefer to look at other infants of their own gender (Kujawski and Bower, 1993).

- Peekaboo is a favorite game at this age, but an adult may need to start the game.

- When an infant is placed together with one other infant, more frequent, complex, and intense peer interaction occurs than when an infant is with many peers.

From Biting to Hugging: Understanding Social Development in Infants and Toddlers

- Infants can understand another's goals and use this awareness to govern their own behavior (Brownell, Ramani, and Zerwas, 2006).

- Children begin to communicate in a variety of ways: actions that pacify, threatening actions, aggressive actions, gestures of fear and retreat, actions that produce isolation (Pines, 1984).

- Peer-directed behaviors of one-year-olds increase dramatically. The conclusion is that toddlers are sophisticated social beings (Kawakami and Takai-Kawakami, 2015).

- Eight-month-old infants selectively prefer characters who act positively toward prosocial individuals and characters who act negatively toward antisocial individuals (Hamlin, Wynn, Bloom, and Mahajan, 2011).

- There is evidence of baby empathy—empathic concern and prosocial behavior in the first year of life for peers (Liddle, Bradley, and Mcgrath, 2015).

- Ten to 20 percent of children eight and ten months of age showed concern for their mothers who were distressed; they showed concern by vocalizing, gesturing, and showing concerned facial expressions (Roth-Hanania, Davidov, and Zahn-Waxler, 2011).

- Children from eight to twelve months of age try to comfort other babies in distress. They smile, make sounds, wave, kick and swing their legs, and shake their heads side to side toward an infant who is crying (Liddle, Bradley, and Mcgrath, 2015).

- Older infants show affection to adults and peers (McMullen et al., 2009).

- Nine-month-olds look to adults to help needy infants (Köster, Ohmer, Nguyen, and Kärtner, 2016).

- Nine- and fourteen-month-olds can make social judgments—infants prefer individuals who treat similar others well and treat dissimilar others poorly (Hamlin, Mahajan, Liberman, and Wynn, 2013).

- Sitting infants may poke, push, or pat another baby to see what that other infant will do. They often look very surprised at the reaction that they get.

- Conflicts occur because of infants' need to explore, interrupted activity, and awakened needs (Licht, Simoni, and Perrig-Chiello, 2008).

- Because infants this age are more goal oriented than in the previous stages, they may push another infant's hand away from a toy or crawl over another baby to get a toy.

12–18 Months

- There is an increase in aggression from twelve to forty-two months (Alink et al., 2006; Tremblay, 2004).

- Toddlers may touch the object that a peer holds. This may be a positive initiation and interactive skill (Eckerman, Whatley, and McGehee, 1979).

- Toddlers show or give a toy to another child (Porter, 2003).

- Toddlers may point to a toy, sharing joint attention with another child (Shin, 2012).

- Toddlers' ability to engage in joint attention at twelve months predicts their social competence at thirty months (Van Hecke et al., 2007).

- Toddlers initiate play with another infant (Porter, 2003).

- Actions are carried out with the intention of attaining a goal; however, goals can change from moment to moment (Jennings, 2004).

- Toddlers communicate using their bodies (Løkken, 2000; Porter, 2003) and in silence and movement (Kultti, 2015).

- Children communicate in a variety of ways: actions that pacify, threatening actions, aggressive actions, gestures of fear and retreat, actions that produce isolation (Pines, 1984).

- Infants share at least twelve themes in their play; for example, they may use positive affect as a meaning sharer. The children use laughter to indicate understanding of each other's actions. They encourage each other to repeat their performances by laughing and/or smiling (Brenner and Mueller, 1982).

- Toddlers are little scientists at this age, experimenting to see how things work. This affects how they get along with peers. They are constantly doing things to other children to see what response they will get.

- Toddlers will imitate each other at this stage; for example, they may make a joyous symphony of spoons banging on the table at mealtime. They communicate with each other by imitating (Trevarthen and Aitken, 2001).

- Children from fourteen to eighteen months old imitate three-step sequences and imitate peers better than they imitate adults (Ryalls, Gul, and Ryalls, 2000; Zmyj, Aschersleben, Prinz, and Daum, 2012).

- Children from fourteen to eighteen months old can imitate peers both five minutes and forty-eight hours after they have observed the peer (who had been taught specific actions with toys) (Hanna and Meltzoff, 1993).

- Between thirteen and fifteen months of age, 27 percent of children engage in complementary and reciprocal play—children demonstrate action-based role reversals in social games such as run and chase or peekaboo displays (Howes and Matheson, 1992).

- Between sixteen and eighteen months of age, 50 percent of children engage in complementary and reciprocal play (run and chase, peekaboo) and 5 percent begin cooperative social pretend play—children enact complementary roles within social pretend play (Howes and Matheson, 1992).

- Toddlers enjoy looking at books together by forming an informal group (this means they move in and out of the group) around the legs, lap, and arms of a favorite parent or teacher.

- Toddlers love sand and water and playing with different sizes of safe bottles and balls. When each has his own bin or tub of water or sand, play goes more smoothly.

- Prosocial behavior is present. Toddlers will retrieve an out-of-reach object accidentally dropped by an adult experimenter (Warneken and Thomasello, 2007).

- Children twelve to eighteen months of age will give their toys to parents with prompting or when reinforced by praise (Parke et al., 2010).

- Children twelve to eighteen months of age will spontaneously warn an adult by pointing out to him an aversive object hidden in his way. Results show that infants intervene spontaneously to help others avoid a problem before it has occurred (Knudsen and Liszkowski, 2013).

- Children sixteen months old take the emotional reactions displayed by novel and previously prosocial sources, but not antisocial sources, into account when deciding what to eat (Hamlin and Wynn, 2012).

- Preferences for another child can begin around twelve months (Howes, 2000).

- Toddler friends exhibit strong preferences for each other and share caring, affective, playful, and humorous relationships (Shin, 2010).

- Toddler friendship is proximity seeking, wanting to be close and to show affection, such as smiling, laughing, and hugging (Whaley and Rubenstein, 1994).

- Toddlers may touch the object that a peer holds. This may be a positive initiation and interactive skill (Eckerman, Whatley, and McGehee, 1979). However, this may lead to conflicts.

- Young toddlers are on the move. For example, in six hours, toddlers take approximately 14,000 steps, walk 46 football fields, and have 100 falls (Adolph et al., 2012). Because they are learning to balance and control their bodies as they walk and have so many falls, they may create conflict when they bump or fall into other children.

- Conflicts occur because of toddlers' need to explore and interrupted activity (Licht, Simoni, and Perrig-Chiello, 2008).

- Biting may appear as toddlers bite others "to see what happens," to get the toy they want, or to express frustration. On the cusp of communicating well, they may communicate through their mouths in the form of a bite.

18–24 Months

- Between nineteen and twenty-three months of age, 56 percent of children play complementary and reciprocal games and 6 percent engage in cooperative social pretend play (Howes and Matheson, 1992).

- Toddlers may have toddler kinesthetic conversations as they follow a leader in moving around the room—moving in and out of the group, taking turns as leader and follower—as if in a conversation of listening and talking, learning valuable turn-taking skills (Løkken, 2000a, 2000b.)

- Toddlers may congregate, cluster, and herd together. When a teacher begins playing an interesting activity with one child, children often come running from the corners of the room.

- Toddlers may work together constructing with blocks—for example, with one the leader and the other the follower (Porter, 2003).

- Children are only beginning to understand that others have preferences different from their own (theory of mind) and are learning to take the perspective of another person.

- Toddlers may work together toward a common goal.

- Toddlers prefer prosocial characters in a cartoon indicating their preference for prosociality (Scola, Holvoet, Arciszewski, and Picard, 2015).

- Children from eighteen to thirty months of age help peers who need help (Hepach, Kante, and Tomasello, 2016).

- Toddlers demonstrate three types of empathy—proximal, altruistic, and self-corrective (Quann and Wein, 2006).

- Children eighteen months old will help adults whether the adult recipient is present or not (Hepach, Haberi, Lambert, and Tomasello, 2017).

- Most toddlers can show kindness to others who are feeling distressed. Toddlers, however, may assume that what will comfort them will also comfort the distressed child. So, the one child may offer his blanket or bottle to the hurt or sad child (Zahn-Waxler, Radke-Yarrow, and King, 1979).

- Some toddlers are capable of offering help to others who are hurt or sad. Some may have an impressive repertoire of altruistic behavior, and if one thing doesn't work they will try another way (Zahn-Waxler, Radke-Yarrow, and King, 1979).

- "Between eighteen and twenty-four months of age, other-oriented resource sharing becomes more frequent, spontaneous, and autonomous, with less need for support and encouragement from the recipient" (Brownell, Iesue, Nichols, and Svetlova, 2013).

- Children from eighteen to twenty-four months divide resources equally. "These results suggest that young children are not selfish, but instead rather generous with resources when they are dividing them among themselves" (Ulber, Hamann, and Tomasello, 2015).

- Friends are more likely to touch, lean on one another, and smile at each other than are children who are not friends.

- Friends prefer each other as interaction partners (Whaley and Rubenstein, 1994).

- Attractive toys may contribute to conflict. If there is only one, more than one child will want to play with it. It is difficult for toddlers to wait their turn.

- Toddlers begin saying *mine* and *yours*. Children who begin saying *mine* between eighteen and twenty-four months of age are more likely to say *yours* and share at twenty-four months (Hay, 2006).

- Toddlers are still learning the differences among the words and concepts of "take turns," "ownership," "possession," "sharing," and "giving."

- Pushing, shoving, grabbing, and hitting may occur as children struggle over "mine for as long as I want it" and "yours, but I want it, too."

- Toddlers may have conflicts over small toys more than large, nonmovable objects (DeStefano and Mueller, 1982).

- Children this age can resist with all their might when another child tries to take a toy.

- Children can focus intently on completing a task such as putting blocks into a container or placing rings on a toy. They may protest when interrupted.

- Conflicts can play a positive role in peer development as children learn that others have ideas that are different from their own and that negotiation needs to occur (Chen, Fein, Killen, and Hak-Ping, 2001); Eckerman and Peterman, 2001; Shantz, 1987).

24–36 Months

- Older toddlers share meaning; for example, types of hits have different meanings to children (Brownlee and Bakeman, 1981).

- Older toddlers are becoming true social partners. The majority of twenty-seven-month-olds could cooperate to accomplish a task (Brownell, Ramani, and Zerwas, 2006).

- Children become more positive and less negative in their social play between twenty-four and thirty-six months (Chen et al., 2001).

- Older toddlers use a variety of words for a variety of functions, such as to describe, explain differences, foster a sense of membership in a social group, and develop a pretend play script (Forman and Hall, 2005b).

- Older toddlers guide other children through prompting, demonstration, and affective signals in relation to a goal (Eckerman and Peterman, 2001).

- Older toddlers can behave prosocially: comforting other children with pats, hugs, and kisses; attempting to remove the cause of another's distress; protecting or warning another child; or suggesting solutions to peer problems (Murphy, 1936).

- By the age of two years, children voluntarily shared valued resources with unrelated individuals when there was no cost to them for doing so. Notably, however, this depended on the recipient making his desire explicit (Brownell, Svetlova, and Nichols, 2009).

- Older toddlers are intrinsically motivated to help others (Hepach, Vaish, and Tomasello, 2012) and are not motivated by extrinsic rewards (Warneken and Tomasello, 2008). Praise that comments on the child's intrinsic motivation, however, is likely to facilitate prosocial behavior (Warneken and Tomasello, 2008).

- Older toddlers begin to understand fairness (Geraci and Surian, 2011).

- Older toddlers were prosocial even when their adult partners were not (Sebastián-Enesco, Hernández-Lloreda, and Colmenares, 2013).

- Older toddlers are caregivers and not just care receivers (Kawakami and Takai-Kawakami, 2015).

- Two-year-olds nurture infants in gentle, respectful ways in a multi-age classroom (McGaha, Cummings, Lippard, and Dallas, 2011).

- Six dimensions are present in two-year-olds friendships: helping, intimacy, loyalty, sharing, similarity, and ritual activity (Whaley and Rubenstein, 1994).

- Children can express glee—they laugh, show delight, and experience joy and hilarity with each other (Løkken, 2000a, 2000b).

- Two- to three-year-olds who were part of a teacher-led training group using storybooks to teach children about emotions displayed gains in emotion understanding (EU) (Grazzani, Ornaghi, Agliati, and Brazzelli, 2016).

- There is a strong relationship between emotion understanding at the age of three and prosocial behavior at the age of four (Ensor, Spencer, and Hughes, 2011).

- Many older toddlers now understand the difference between "ownership" and "possession" (Fasig, 2000); however, it is still difficult for them to control their urge to play with an attractive toy that another child has in his possession.

- Children twenty-four to thirty months old understood the term *ownership*. They said *mine* to items they owned and *yours* to items other children owned (Ross, Friedman, and Field, 2015).

- There is a reduction in conflict over objects (Chen, 2001).

- Children use many strategies during conflicts (Hay, 2006). They might insist, reason, offer alternative proposals, compromise, ignore, request an explanation, or use physical force (Chen, 2001). They raise their voices, talk faster, and emphasize certain points (Brenneis and Lein, 1977).

- One child's dominance over another can occur (Hawley and Little, 1999).

- Biting occurs for many reasons, a primary one being that children are learning to "use their words" and take another person's perspective (Wittmer and Petersen, 2017).

- Children who are aggressive need support to feel safe, learn alternative strategies, and have access to early intervention or mental-health services.

- Among high-risk toddlers, aggression is a predictor of poor school-age academic achievement (Brennan, Shaw, Dishion, and Wilson, 2012).

References and Recommended Reading

Adolph, Karen, et al. 2012. "How Do You Learn to Walk? Thousands of Steps and Dozens of Falls Per Day." *Psychological Science* 23(11): 1387–1394.

Ainsworth, Mary, Mary Blehar, Everett Waters, and Sally Wall. 1978. *Patterns of Attachment: A Psychological Study of the Strange Situation.* Hillsdale, NJ: Erlbaum.

Alink, Lenneke, et al. 2006. "The Early Childhood Aggression Curve: Development of Physical Aggression in 10- to 50-Month-Old Children." *Child Development* 77(4): 954–966.

Astington, Janet, and Margaret Edward. 2010. "The Development of Theory of Mind in Early Childhood." In *Encyclopedia on Early Childhood Development* [online]. Montréal, QC: Centre of Excellence for Early Childhood Development and the Strategic Knowledge Cluster on Early Child Development. http://www.child-encyclopedia.com/social-cognition/according-experts/development-theory-mind-early-childhood

Baillargeon, Raymond, Gregory Sward, Kate Keenan, and Guanqiong Cao. 2011. "Opposition-Defiance in the Second Year of Life: A Population-Based Cohort Study." *Infancy* 16(4): 418–434.

Baillargeon, Raymond, et al. 2007. "Gender Differences in Physical Aggression: A Prospective Population-Based Survey of Children Before and After Two Years of Age." *Developmental Psychology* 43(1): 13–26.

Bandura, Albert. 1989. "Social Cognitive Theory." In *Annals of Child Development, Volume 6.* Greenwich, CT: JAI Press.

Bayer, Cherie, Kimberlee Whaley, and Stephen May. 1995. "Strategic Assistance in Toddler Disputes II: Sequences and Patterns of Teachers' Message Strategies." *Early Education and Development* 6(4): 406–432.

Belacchi, Carmen, and Eleonora Farina. 2012. "Feeling and Thinking of Others: Affective and Cognitive Empathy and Emotion Comprehension in Prosocial/Hostile Preschoolers." *Aggressive Behavior* 38(2): 150–165.

Benzies, Karen, Leslie Anne Keown, and Joyce Magill-Evans. 2009. "Immediate and Sustained Effects of Parenting on Physical Aggression in Canadian Children Aged 6 Years and Younger." *Canadian Journal of Psychiatry* 54(1): 55–64.

Bernard, Kristen, E. B. Meade, and Mary Dozier. 2013. "Parental Synchrony and Nurturance as Targets in an Attachment-Based Intervention: Building upon Mary Ainsworth's Insights about Mother-Infant Interaction." *Attachment and Human Development* 15(5): 507–523.

Blandon, Alysia, and Meghan Scrimgeour. 2015. "Child, Parenting, and Situational Characteristics Associated with Toddlers' Prosocial Behaviour." *Infant and Child Development* 24(6): 643–660.

Bowlby, John. 1988. *A Secure Base: Parent-Child Attachment and Healthy Human Development.* New York: Basic Books.

Bradley, Benjamin S., and Jane Selby. 2004. "Observing Infants in Groups: The Clan Revisited." *Infant Observation* 7(2–3): 107–122.

Bradley, Benjamin S., and Michael Smithson. 2017. "Groupness in Preverbal Infants: Proof of Concept." *Frontiers in Psychology* 8: 385. https://www.ncbi.nlm.nih.gov/pmc/articles/PMC5352679/

Brennan, Lauretta, Daniel Shaw, Thomas Dishion, and Melvin Wilson. 2012. "Longitudinal Predictors of School-Age Academic Achievement: Unique Contributions of Toddler-Age Aggression, Oppositionality, Inattention, and Hyperactivity." *Journal of Abnormal Child Psychology* 40(8): 1289–1300.

Brenneis, Donald, and Laura Lein. 1977. "'You Fruithead': A Sociolinguistic Approach to Dispute Settlement." In *Child Discourse*. New York: Academic Press.

Brenner, Jeffrey, and Edward Mueller. 1982. "Shared Meaning in Boy Toddlers' Peer Relations." *Child Development* 53(2): 380–391.

Briggs, Dorothy. 1988. *Your Child's Self-Esteem*. New York: Broadway Books.

Brooks, Jeanne, and Michael Lewis. 1976. "Infants' Responses to Strangers: Midget, Adult, and Child." *Child Development* 47(2): 323–332.

Brophy-Herb, Holly, et al. 2011. "Toddlers' Social-Emotional Competence in the Contexts of Maternal Emotion Socialization and Contingent Responsiveness in a Low-Income Sample." *Social Development* 20(1): 73–92.

Brownell, Celia. 2012. "Early Development of Prosocial Behavior: Current Perspectives." *Infancy* 18(1): 1–9.

Brownell, Celia, Stephanie Iesue, Sara Nichols, and Margarita Svetlova. 2013. "Mine or Yours? Development of Sharing in Toddlers in Relation to Ownership Understanding." *Child Development* 84(3): 906–920.

Brownell, Celia, Geetha Ramani, and Stephanie Zerwas. 2006. "Becoming a Social Partner with Peers: Cooperation and Social Understanding in One- and Two-Year-Olds." *Child Development* 77(4): 803–821.

Brownell, Celia, Margarita Svetlova, and Sara Nichols. 2009. "To Share or Not to Share: When Do Toddlers Respond to Another's Needs?" *Infancy* 14(1): 117–130.

Brownlee, John, and Roger Bakeman. 1981. "Hitting in Toddler-Peer Interaction." *Child Development* 52(3): 1076–1079.

Bruner, Jerome. 1996. *The Culture of Education*. Boston, MA: Harvard University Press.

Buss, Kristin, et al. 2013. "Dysregulated Fear Predicts Social Wariness and Social Anxiety Symptoms during Kindergarten." *Journal of Clinical Child and Adolescent Psychology* 42(5): 603–616.

Campbell, Susan, Susan Spieker, Margaret Burchinal, and Michele Poe. 2006. "Trajectories of Aggression from Toddlerhood to Age 9 Predict Academic and Social Functioning through Age 12." *Journal of Child Psychology and Psychiatry* 47(8): 791–800.

Center on the Developing Child. 2017a. *Brain Architecture*. Harvard University. http://developingchild.harvard.edu/science/key-concepts/brain-architecture/

Center on the Developing Child. 2017b. *8 Things to Remember about Child Development*. Harvard University. http://developingchild.harvard.edu/resources/8-things-remember-child-development/

Center on the Developing Child 2017c. *Five Numbers to Remember about Early Childhood Development*. Harvard University. http://developingchild.harvard.edu/resources/five-numbers-to-remember-about-early-childhood-development/

Center on the Developing Child. 2017d. *InBrief: The Impact of Early Adversity on Children's Development*. Harvard University. http://developingchild.harvard.edu/resources/inbrief-the-impact-of-early-adversity-on-childrens-development-video/

Center on the Developing Child. 2017e. *Serve and Return*. Harvard University. http://developingchild.harvard.edu/science/key-concepts/serve-and-return/

Cheah, Charissa, and Kenneth Rubin. 2004. "European American and Mainland Chinese Mothers' Responses to Aggression and Social Withdrawal in Preschoolers." *International Journal of Behavioral Development* 28(1): 83–94.

Chen, Dora. 2003. "Preventing Violence by Promoting the Development of Competent Conflict Resolution Skills: Exploring Roles and Responsibilities." *Early Childhood Education Journal* 30(4): 203–208.

Chen, Dora, Greta Fein, Melanie Killen, and Tam Hak-Ping. 2001. "Peer Conflicts of Preschool Children: Issues, Resolution, Incidence, and Age-Related Patterns." *Early Education and Development* 12(4): 523–544.

Christopher, Caroline, et al. 2013. "Maternal Empathy and Changes in Mothers' Permissiveness as Predictors of Toddlers' Early Social Competence with Peers: A Parenting Intervention Study." *Journal of Child and Family Studies* 22(6): 769–778.

Colorado EQ Project. 2017. *Module—Care of the Spirit*. Denver, CO: Colorado Department of Education.

Côté, Sylvana, et al. 2006. "The Development of Physical Aggression from Toddlerhood to Pre-Adolescence: A Nationwide Longitudinal Study of Canadian Children." *Journal of Abnormal Child Psychology* 34(1): 71–86.

Crockenberg, Susan, Esther Leerkes, and Shamila Lekka. 2007. "Pathways from Marital Aggression to Infant Emotion Regulation: The Development of Withdrawal in Infancy." *Infant Behavior and Development* 30(1): 97–113.

Cryer, Debby, et al. 2005. "Effects of Transitions to New Child Care Classes on Infant/Toddler Distress and Behavior." *Early Childhood Research Quarterly* 20(1): 37–56.

Dahl, Audun. 2015. "The Developing Social Context of Infant Helping in Two U.S. Samples." *Child Development* 86(4): 1080–1093.

Dahl Audun. 2016. "Mothers' Insistence when Prohibiting Infants from Harming Others in Everyday Interactions." *Frontiers in Psychology* 7: 1448.

DaRos, Denise, and Beverly Kovach. 1998. "Assisting Toddlers and Caregivers during Conflict Resolutions: Interactions that Promote Socialization." *Childhood Education* 75(1): 25–30.

Davidov, Maayan, Carolyn Zahn-Waxler, Ronit Roth-Hanania, and Ariel Knafo. 2013. "Concern for Others in the First Year of Life: Theory, Evidence, and Avenues for Research." *Child Development Perspectives* 7(2): 126–131.

Davies, Patrick, Dante Cicchetti, and Meredith Martin. 2012. "Toward Greater Specificity in Identifying Associations among Interparental Aggression, Child Emotional Reactivity to Conflict, and Child Problems." *Child Development* 83(5): 1789–1804.

Davis, Belinda, and Sheila Degotardi. 2015. "Educators' Understandings of, and Support for, Infant Peer Relationships in Early Childhood Settings." *Journal of Early Childhood Research* 13(1): 64–78.

Dennis, Tracy, Melanie Hong, and Beylul Solomon. 2010. "Do the Associations between Exuberance and Emotion Regulation Depend on Effortful Control?" *International Journal of Behavioral Development* 34(5): 462–472.

DeStefano, Charles, and Edward Mueller. 1982. "Environmental Determinants of Peer Social Activity in 18-Month-Old Males." *Infant Behavior and Development* 5(2–4): 175–183.

Deynoot-Schaub, Mirjam, and J. Marianne Riksen-Walraven. 2006. "Peer Interaction in Child Care Centres at 15 and 23 Months: Stability and Links with Children's Socio-Emotional Adjustment." *Infant Behavior and Development* 29(2): 276–288.

Dollar, Jessica, and Kristin Buss. 2014. "Approach and Positive Affect in Toddlerhood Predict Early Childhood Behavior Problems." *Social Development* 23(2): 267–287.

Domitrovich, Celine, Rebecca Cortes, and Mark Greenberg. 2007. "Improving Young Children's Social and Emotional Competence: A Randomized Trial of the Preschool PATHS Curriculum." *The Journal of Primary Prevention* 28(2): 67–91.

Drummond, Jesse, et al. 2016. "Helping the One You Hurt: Toddlers' Rudimentary Guilt, Shame, and Prosocial Behavior after Harming Another." *Child Development* 88(4): 1382–1397.

Dunfield, Kristen, and Valerie Kuhlmeier. 2010. "Intention Mediated Selective Helping in Human Infants." *Psychological Science* 21(4): 523–527.

Ebbeck, Marjory, et al. 2015. "A Research Study on Secure Attachment Using the Primary Caregiving Approach." *Early Childhood Education Journal* 43(3): 233–240.

Eckerman, Carol, and Karen Peterman. 2001. "Peers and Infant Social/Communicative Development." In *Blackwell Handbook of Infant Development*. Malden, MA: Blackwell.

Eckerman, Carol, J. L. Whatley, and L. J. McGehee. 1979. "Approaching and Contacting the Object Another Manipulates: A Social Skill of the One-Year-Old." *Developmental Psychology* 15: 585–593.

Ensor, Rosie, and Claire Hughes. 2008. "Content or Connectedness? Mother-Child Talk and Early Social Understanding." *Child Development* 79(1): 201–216.

Ensor, Rosie, Debra Spencer, and Claire Hughes. 2011. "'You Feel Sad?' Emotion Understanding Mediates Effects of Verbal Ability and Mother-Child Mutuality on Prosocial Behaviors: Findings from 2 Years to 4 Years." *Social Development* 20(1): 93–110.

Fasig, Lauren. 2000. "Toddlers' Understanding of Ownership: Implications for Self-Concept Development." *Social Development* 9(3): 370–382.

Fernald, Anne, and Adriana Weisleder. 2015. "Twenty Years after *Meaningful Differences*, It Is Time to Reframe the 'Deficit' Debate about the Importance of Children's Early Language Experience." *Human Development* 58(1): 1–4.

Forman, George, and Ellen Hall. 2005a. *It Takes to Give*. Amherst, MA: Videatives. https://videatives.com/node/1703

Forman, George, and Ellen Hall. 2005b. *Social Clay*. Amherst, MA: Videatives. https://videatives.com/node/1768

Fox, Nathan, et al. 2013. "Commentary: To Intervene or Not? Appreciating or Treating Individual Differences in Childhood Temperament." *Journal of Child Psychology and Psychiatry* 54(7): 789–790.

Gazelle, Heidi. 2006. "Class Climate Moderates Peer Relations and Emotional Adjustment in Children with an Early History of Anxious Solitude: A Child x Environment Model." *Developmental Psychology* 42(6): 1179–1192.

Gazelle, Heidi. 2010. "Anxious Solitude/Withdrawal and Anxiety Disorders: Conceptualization, Co-Occurrence, and Peer Processes Leading Toward and Away from Disorder in Childhood." In *Social Anxiety in Childhood: Bridging Developmental and Clinical Perspectives, no. 127*. San Francisco, CA: Jossey-Bass.

Geraci, Alessandra, and Luca Surian. 2011. "The Developmental Roots of Fairness: Infants' Reactions to Equal and Unequal Distributions of Resources." *Developmental Science* 14(5): 1012–1020.

Gillespie, Linda, and Amy Hunter. 2010. "Believe, Watch, Act! Promoting Prosocial Behavior in Infants and Toddlers." *Young Children* 65(1): 42–43.

Gloeckler, Lissy, and Jennifer Cassell. 2012. "Teacher Practices with Toddlers during Social Problem Solving Opportunities." *Early Childhood Education Journal* 40(4): 251–257.

Grazzani, Ilaria, Veronica Ornaghi, Alessia Agliati, and Elisa Brazzelli. 2016. "How to Foster Toddlers' Mental-State Talk, Emotion Understanding, and Prosocial Behavior: A Conversation-Based Intervention at Nursery School." *Infancy* 21(2): 199–227.

Groeneveld, Marleen, Harriet Vermeer, Marinus van IJzendoorn, and Mariëlle Linting. 2012. "Stress, Cortisol, and Well-Being of Caregivers and Children in Home-Based Child Care: A Case for Differential Susceptibility." *Child: Care, Health, and Development* 38(2): 251–260.

Groh, Ashley, et al. 2014. "The Significance of Attachment Security for Children's Social Competence with Peers: A Meta-Analytic Study." *Attachment and Human Development* 16(2): 103–136.

Gromoske, Andrea, and Kathryn Maguire-Jack. 2012. "Transactional and Cascading Relations between Early Spanking and Children's Social-Emotional Development." *Journal of Marriage and Family* 74(5): 1054–1068.

Gross, Rebekkah, et al. 2015. "Individual Differences in Toddlers' Social Understanding and Prosocial Behavior: Disposition or Socialization?" *Frontiers in Psychology* 6: 1–11.

Guedeney, Antoine, et al. 2014. "Social Withdrawal at 1 Year Is Associated with Emotional and Behavioural Problems at 3 and 5 Years: The Eden Mother-Child Cohort Study." *European Child and Adolescent Psychiatry* 23(12): 1181–1188.

Gunnar, Megan, Erin Kryzer, Mark Van Ryzin, and Deborah Phillips. 2010. "The Rise in Cortisol in Family Day Care: Associations with Aspects of Care Quality, Child Behavior, and Sex." *Child Development* 81(3): 851–869.

Gunnar, Megan, and Regina Sullivan. 2017. "The Neurodevelopment of Social Buffering and Fear Learning: Integration and Crosstalk." *Social Neuroscience* 12(1): 1–7.

Hall, Ellen, and George Forman. n.d. *Gracious Toddler: It Was Mine, but Let Me Help.* Amherst, MA: Videatives. https://videatives.com/node/1847

Hamlin, J. Kiley. 2014. "Context-Dependent Social Evaluation in 4.5-Month-Old Human Infants: The Role of Domain-General versus Domain-Specific Processes in the Development of Social Evaluation." *Frontiers in Psychology* 5: 1–10.

Hamlin, J. Kiley, Neha Mahajan, Zoe Liberman, and Karen Wynn. 2013. "Not Like Me = Bad: Infants Prefer Those Who Harm Dissimilar Others." *Psychological Science* 24(4): 589–594.

Hamlin, J. Kiley, and Karen Wynn. 2011. "Young Infants Prefer Prosocial to Antisocial Others." *Cognitive Development* 26(1): 30–39.

Hamlin, J. Kiley, and Karen Wynn. 2012. "Who Knows What's Good to Eat? Infants Fail to Match the Food Preferences of Antisocial Others." *Cognitive Development* 27(3): 227–239.

Hamlin, J. Kiley, Karen Wynn, and Paul Bloom. 2007. "Social Evaluation by Preverbal Infants." *Nature* 450(7169): 557–559.

Hamlin, J. Kiley, Karen Wynn, and Paul Bloom. 2010. "Three-Month-Olds Show a Negativity Bias in Their Social Evaluations." *Developmental Science* 13(6): 923–929.

Hamlin, J. Kiley, Karen Wynn, Paul Bloom, and Neha Mahajan. 2011. "How Infants and Toddlers React to Antisocial Others." *Proceedings of the National Academy of Sciences of the United States of America* 108(50): 19931–19936.

Hanna, Elizabeth, and Andrew Meltzoff. 1993. "Peer Imitation by Toddlers in Laboratory, Home, and Day-Care Contexts: Implications for Social Learning and Memory." *Developmental Psychology* 29(4): 701–710.

Hart, Betty, and Todd Risley. 1995. *Meaningful Differences in the Everyday Experience of Young American Children.* Baltimore, MD: Paul H. Brookes.

Hawley, Patricia, and Todd Little. 1999. "On Winning Some and Losing Some: A Social Relations Approach to Social Dominance in Toddlers." *Merrill-Palmer Quarterly* 45(2): 185–214.

Hay, Dale. 2006. "Yours and Mine: Toddlers' Talk about Possessions with Familiar Peers." *British Journal of Developmental Psychology* 24(1): 39–52.

Hay, Dale, and Hildy Ross. 1982. "The Social Nature of Early Conflict." *Child Development* 53(1): 105–113.

Hay, Dale, Sarah-Louise Hurst, Cerith Waters, and Andrea Chadwick. 2011. "Infants' Use of Force to Defend Toys: The Origins of Instrumental Aggression." *Infancy* 16(5): 471–489.

Hay, Dale, et al. 2010. "Identifying Early Signs of Aggression: Psychometric Properties of the Cardiff Infant Contentiousness Scale." *Aggressive Behavior* 36(6): 351–357.

Hay, Dale, et al. 2011. "The Emergence of Gender Differences in Physical Aggression in the Context of Conflict between Young Peers." *British Journal of Developmental Psychology* 29(2): 158–175.

Hay, Dale, et al. 2014. "Precursors to Aggression Are Evident by 6 Months of Age." *Developmental Science* 17(3): 471–480.

Heberle, Amy, et al. 2014. "The Impact of Neighborhood, Family, and Individual Risk Factors on Toddlers' Disruptive Behavior." *Child Development* 85(5): 2046–2061.

Hedenbro, Monica, and Per-Anders Rydelius. 2014. "Early Interaction between Infants and Their Parents Predicts Social Competence at the Age of Four." *Acta Paediatrica* 103(3): 268–274.

Heitler, Susan. 2011. "Discipline with Babies and Toddlers." *Psychology Today*. https://www.psychologytoday.com/blog/resolution-not-conflict/201110/discipline-babies-and-toddlers

Henderson, Heather, Peter Marshall, Nathan Fox, and Kenneth Rubin. 2004. "Psychophysiological and Behavioral Evidence for Varying Forms and Functions of Nonsocial Behavior in Preschoolers." *Child Development* 75(1): 251–263.

Hepach, Robert, Katharina Haberl, Stéphane Lambert, and Michael Tomasello. 2017. "Toddlers Help Anonymously." *Infancy* 22(1): 130–145.

Hepach, Robert, Nadine Kante, and Michael Tomasello. 2016. "Toddlers Help a Peer." *Child Development*. doi: 10.1111/cdev.12686

Hepach, Robert, Amrisha Vaish, and Michael Tomasello, M. 2012. "Young Children Are Intrinsically Motivated to See Others Helped." *Psychological Science* 23(9): 967–972.

Hepach, Robert, Amrisha Vaish, and Michael Tomasello. 2013. "Young Children Sympathize Less in Response to Unjustified Emotional Distress." *Development Psychology* 49(6): 1132–1138.

Hinde, Robert. 1992. "Ethological and Relationship Approaches." In *Six Theories of Child Development: Revised Formulations and Current Issues*. London, UK: Jessica Kingsley Publishers.

Holden, George, Alan Brown, Austin Baldwin, and Kathryn Croft Caderao. 2014. "Research Findings Can Change Attitudes about Corporal Punishment." *Child Abuse and Neglect* 38(5): 902–908.

Honig, Alice. 2014. *The Best for Babies: Expert Advice for Assessing Infant-Toddler Programs*. Lewisville, NC: Gryphon House.

Honig, Alice, and Alyce Thompson. 1994. "Helping Toddlers with Peer-Group Entry Skills." *Zero to Three* 14(5): 15–19.

Howard, Lauren, Annette Henderson, Cristina Carrazza, and Amanda Woodward. 2015. "Infants' and Young Children's Imitation of Linguistic In-Group and Out-Group Informants." *Child Development* 86(1): 259–275.

Howes, Carollee. 1988. "Peer Interaction of Young Children." *Monographs of the Society for Research in Child Development* 53(1). Hoboken, NJ: John Wiley and Sons.

Howes, Carollee. 2000. "Social Development, Family, and Attachment Relationships." In *Infants and Toddlers in Out-of-Home Care*. Baltimore, MD: Paul H. Brookes.

Howes, Carollee, and Joann Farver. 1992. "Toddlers' Responses to the Distress of Their Peers." *Journal of Applied Developmental Psychology* 8(4): 441–452.

Howes, Carollee, Claire Hamilton, and Catherine Matheson. 1994. "Children's Relationships with Peers: Differential Associations with Aspects of the Teacher-Child Relationship." *Child Development* 65(1): 253–263.

Howes, Carollee, and Catherine Matheson. 1992. "Sequences in the Development of Competent Play with Peers: Social and Social Pretend Play." *Developmental Psychology* 28(5): 961–974.

Hutt, Rachel, Kristin Buss, and Elizabeth Kiel. 2013. "Caregiver Protective Behavior, Toddler Fear and Sadness, and Toddler Cortisol Reactivity in Novel Contexts." *Infancy* 18(5): 708–728.

Hymel, Shelley, and Laurie Ford. 2014. "School Completion and Academic Success: The Impact of Early Social-Emotional Competence." *Encyclopedia on Early Childhood Development*. http://www.child-encyclopedia.com/school-success/according-experts/school-completion-and-academic-success-impact-early-social

Hyson, Marilou, and Jackie Taylor. 2011. "Caring about Caring: What Adults Can Do to Promote Young Children's Prosocial Skills." *Young Children* 66(4): 74–83.

Jennings, Kay. 2004. "Development of Goal-Directed Behavior and Related Self-Processes in Toddlers." *International Journal of Behavioral Development* 28(4): 319–327.

Johnson, James, James Christie, and Thomas Yawkey. 1998. *Play and Early Childhood Development*. 2nd ed. New York: Longman.

Jones, Damon, Mark Greenberg, and Max Crowley. 2015. "Early Social-Emotional Functioning and Public Health: The Relationship between Kindergarten Social Competence and Future Wellness." *American Journal of Public Health* 105(11): 2283–2290.

Kaplan, Louise. 1978. *Oneness and Separateness*. New York: Simon and Schuster.

Kawakami, Kiyobumi, and Kiyoko Takai-Kawakami. 2015. "Teaching, Caring, and Altruistic Behaviors in Toddlers." *Infant Behavior and Development* 41: 108–112.

Kelly, Jean, Tracy Zuckerman, Diana Sandoval, and Kim Buehlman. 2001. *Promoting First Relationships: A Program for Service Providers to Help Parents and Other Caregivers Nurture Young Children's Social and Emotional Development*. Seattle, WA: Nursing Child Assessment Satellite Training Programs, University of Washington Publications.

Kiel, Elizabeth, Julie Premo, and Kristin Buss. 2016. "Maternal Encouragement to Approach Novelty: A Curvilinear Relation to Change in Anxiety for Inhibited Toddlers." *Journal of Abnormal Child Psychology* 44(3): 433–444.

Kim, Sanghag, and Grazyna Kochanska. 2012. "Child Temperament Moderates Effects of Parent-Child Mutuality on Self-Regulation: A Relationship-Based Path for Emotionally Negative Infants." *Child Development* 83(4): 1275–1289.

Kim, Sonia de Groot. 2010. "There's Elly, It Must Be Tuesday: Discontinuity in Child Care Programs and Its Impact on the Development of Peer Relationships in Young Children." *Early Childhood Education Journal* 38(2): 153–164.

Kirk, Elizabeth, et al. 2015. "A Longitudinal Investigation of the Relationship between Maternal Mind-Mindedness and Theory of Mind. *British Journal of Developmental Psychology* 33(4): 434–445.

Klein, Benjamin, Jan Willem Gorter, and Peter Rosenbaum. 2013. "Diagnostic Shortfalls in Early Childhood Chronic Stress: A Review of the Issues." *Child: Care, Health and Development* 39(6): 765–771.

Knudsen, Birgit, and Ulf Liszkowski. 2013. "One-Year-Olds Warn Others about Negative Action Outcomes." *Journal of Cognition and Development* 14(3): 424–436.

Kobiella, Andrea, Tobias Grossmann, Vincent Reid, and Tricia Striano. 2008. "The Discrimination of Angry and Fearful Facial Expressions in 7-Month-Old Infants: An Event-Related Potential Study." *Cognition and Emotion* 22(1): 134–146.

Kochanska, Grazyna, and Sanghag Kim. 2012. "Toward a New Understanding of Legacy of Early Attachments for Future Antisocial Trajectories: Evidence from Two Longitudinal Studies." *Development and Psychopathology* 24(3): 783–806.

Kochanska, Grazyna, and Sanghag Kim. 2013. "Early Attachment Organization with Both Parents and Future Behavior Problems: From Infancy to Middle Childhood." *Child Development* 84(1): 283–296.

Koplow, Lesley, ed. 1996. *Unsmiling Faces: How Preschools Can Heal.* New York: Teachers College Press.

Köster, Moritz, et al. 2016. "Cultural Influences on Toddlers' Prosocial Behavior: How Maternal Task Assignment Relates to Helping Others." *Child Development* 87(6): 1727–1738.

Köster, Moritz, Xenia Ohmer, Thanh Dung Nguyen, and Joscha Kärtner. 2016. "Infants Understand Others' Needs." *Psychological Science* 27(4): 542–548.

Kujawski, Jacqueline, and T. G. R. Bower. 1993. "Same-Sex Preferential Looking during Infancy as a Function of Abstract Representation." *British Journal of Developmental Psychology* 11(2): 201–209.

Kultti, Anne. 2015. "Adding Learning Resources: A Study of Two Toddlers' Modes and Trajectories of Participation in Early Childhood Education." *International Journal of Early Years Education* 23(2): 209–221.

La Paro, Karen, and Lissy Gloeckler. 2016. "The Context of Child Care for Toddlers: The 'Experience Expectable Environment.'" *Early Childhood Education Journal* 44(2): 147–153.

Lauw, Michelle, et al. 2014. "Improving Parenting of Toddlers' Emotions Using an Emotion Coaching Parenting Program: A Pilot Study of Tuning In to Toddlers." *Journal of Community Psychology* 42(2): 169–175.

Lee, Shawna, Inna Altschul, and Elizabeth Gershoff. 2013. "Does Warmth Moderate Longitudinal Associations between Maternal Spanking and Child Aggression in Early Childhood?" *Developmental Psychology* 49(11): 2017–2028.

Legendre, Alain, and Dominique Munchenbach. 2011. "Two-to-Three-Year-Old Children's Interactions with Peers in Child-Care Centres: Effects of Spatial Distance to Caregivers." *Infant Behavior and Development* 34(1): 111–125.

Lewis-Morrarty, Erin, et al. 2015. "Infant Attachment Security and Early Childhood Behavioral Inhibition Interact to Predict Adolescent Social Anxiety Symptoms." *Child Development* 86(2): 598–613.

Licht, Batya, Heidi Simoni, and Pasqualina Perrig-Chiello. 2008. "Conflict between Peers in Infancy and Toddler Age: What Do They Fight About? *Early Years: Journal of International Research and Development* 28(3): 235–249.

Liddle, Mitzi-Jane, Ben Bradley, and Andrew Mcgrath. 2015. "Baby Empathy: Infant Distress and Peer Prosocial Responses." *Infant Mental Health Journal* 36(4): 446–458.

Lieberman, Alicia. 1993. *The Emotional Life of the Toddler.* New York: Free Press.

Lillvist, Anne. 2005. "Observations of Social Competence in the Preschool—A Comparison of Children in Need of Special Support and Typically Developing Children." Diss. Mälardalen University. Västerås, Sweden. Available from anne.lillvist@mdh.se

Løkken, Gunvor. 2000a. "The Playful Quality of the Toddling 'Style.'" *International Journal of Qualitative Studies in Education* 13(5): 531–542

Løkken, Gunvor. 2000b. "Tracing the Social Style of Toddler Peers." *Scandinavian Journal of Educational Research* 44(2): 163–176.

McElwain, Nancy, et al. 2008. "A Process Model of Attachment-Friend Linkages: Hostile Attribution Biases, Language Ability, and Mother-Child Affective Mutuality as Intervening Mechanisms." *Child Development* 79(6): 1891–1906.

McElwain, Nancy, Martha Cox, Margaret Burchinal, and Jenny Macfie. 2003. "Differentiating among Insecure Mother-Infant Attachment Classifications: A Focus on Child-Friend Interaction and Exploration during Solitary Play at 36 Months." *Attachment and Human Development* 5(2): 136–164.

McGaha, Cindy, Rebekah Cummings, Barbara Lippard, and Karen Dallas. 2011. "Relationships Building: Infants, Toddlers, and 2-Year-Olds." *Early Childhood Research and Practice* 13(1). http://ecrp.uiuc.edu/v13n1/mcgaha.html

McMullen, Mary, et al. 2009. "Learning to Be *Me* while Coming to Understand *We*: Encouraging Prosocial Babies in Group Settings." *Young Children* 64(4): 20–28.

Meltzoff, Andrew. 2007. "The 'Like Me' Framework for Recognizing and Becoming an Intentional Agent." *Acta Psychologica* 124(1): 26–43.

Meltzoff, Andrew. 2011. "Social Cognition and the Origins of Imitation, Empathy, and Theory of Mind." In *The Wiley-Blackwell Handbook of Childhood Cognitive Development*. 2nd ed. Malden, MA: Wiley-Blackwell.

Miller, Alison, Ronald Seifer, Rebecca Crossin, and Monique Lebourgeois. 2015. "Toddler's Self-Regulation Strategies in a Challenge Context Are Nap-Dependent." *Journal of Sleep Research* 24(3): 279–287.

Murphy, Lois. 1936. "Sympathetic Behavior in Young Children." *Journal of Experimental Education* 5(1): 79–90.

Nadel, Jacqueline, C. Guérini, A. Pezé, and C. Rivet. 1999. "The Evolving Nature of Imitation as a Transitory Means of Communication." In *Imitation in Infancy*. Cambridge, MA: Cambridge University Press.

National Institute of Child Health and Human Development. 2001. "Child Care and Children's Peer Interaction at 24 and 36 Months: The NICHD Study of Early Child Care." *Child Development* 72(5): 1478–1500.

National Scientific Council on the Developing Child. 2004. *Young Children Develop in an Environment of Relationships: Working Paper No. 1*. http://developingchild.harvard.edu/wp-content/uploads/2004/04/Young-Children-Develop-in-an-Environment-of-Relationships.pdf

National Scientific Council on the Developing Child. 2005/2014. *Excessive Stress Disrupts the Architecture of the Developing Brain: Working Paper No. 3*. Updated Edition. http://46y5eh11fhgw3ve3ytpwxt9r.wpengine.netdna-cdn.com/wp-content/uploads/2005/05/Stress_Disrupts_Architecture_Developing_Brain-1.pdf

National Scientific Council on the Developing Child. 2010. *Persistent Fear and Anxiety Can Affect Young Children's Learning and Development: Working Paper No. 9*. http://46y5eh11fhgw3ve3ytpwxt9r.wpengine.netdna-cdn.com/wp-content/uploads/2010/05/Persistent-Fear-and-Anxiety-Can-Affect-Young-Childrens-Learning-and-Development.pdf

Newton, Emily, Ross Thompson, and Miranda Goodman. 2016. "Individual Differences in Toddlers' Prosociality: Experiences in Early Relationships Explain Variability in Prosocial Behavior." *Child Development* 87(6): 1715–1726.

Nichols, Sara, Margarita Svetlova, and Celia Brownell. 2009. "The Role of Social Understanding and Empathic Disposition in Young Children's Responsiveness to Distress in Parents and Peers." *Cognition, Brain, Behavior* 13(4): 449–478.

Nichols, Sara, Margarita Svetlova, and Celia Brownell. 2015. "Toddlers' Responses to Infants' Negative Emotions." *Infancy* 20(1): 70–97.

Nygren, Maria, John Carstensen, Johnny Ludvigsson, and Anneli Sepa Frostell. 2012. "Adult Attachment and Parenting Stress among Parents of Toddlers." *Journal of Reproductive and Infant Psychology* 30(3): 289–302.

Ødegaard, Elin Ekiksen. 2006. "What's Worth Talking About? Meaning-Making in Toddler-Initiated Conarratives in Preschool." *Early Years* 26(1): 79–92.

Osofsky, Joy D. 2002. "Helping Young Children and Families Cope with Trauma in a New Era." *Zero to Three* 22(3): 18–20.

Over, Harriet, and Malinda Carpenter. 2012. "Putting the Social into Social Learning: Explaining Both Selectivity and Fidelity in Children's Copying Behavior." *Journal of Comparative Psychology* 126(2): 182–192.

Parke, Ross D., and Alison Clarke-Stewart. 2010. *Social Development*. Hoboken, NJ: John Wiley and Sons.

Parten, Mildred B. 1932. "Social Participation among Preschool Children." *Journal of Abnormal and Social Psychology* 27: 243–269.

Paulus, Markus. 2014. "The Emergence of Prosocial Behavior: Why Do Infants and Toddlers Help, Comfort, and Share?" *Child Development Perspective* 8(2): 77–81.

Paulus, Markus, and Chris Moore. 2012. "Producing and Understanding Prosocial Actions in Early Childhood." *Advances in Child Development and Behavior* 42: 271–305.

Peth-Pierce, Robin. 2000. "A Good Beginning: Sending America's Children to School with the Social and Emotional Competence They Need to Succeed." Bethesda, MD: National Institute of Mental Health. https://scholar.google.com/citations?view_op=view_citationandhl=enanduser=e3b-mfgAAAAJandcitation_for_view=e3b-mfgAAAAJ:d1gkVwhDpl0C

Piaget, Jean. 1936/1953. *The Origins of Intelligence in the Child*. New York: International Universities Press.

Piaget, Jean. 1952. *The Origins of Intelligence in Children*. New York: Norton.

Pines, Maya. 1979. "Good Samaritans at Age Two?" *Psychology Today* 13: 66–74.

Pines, Maya. 1984. "Children's Winning Ways." *Psychology Today* 18: 59–65.

Porter, Phyllis. 2003. "Social Relationships of Infants in Daycare." Educarer. http://www.educarer.com/current-article-relationships.htm

Quann, Valerie, and Carol Anne Wien. 2006. "The Visible Empathy of Infants and Toddlers." *Young Children* 61(4): 22–29.

Razza, Rachel, Anne Martin, and Jeanne Brooks-Gunn. 2012. "Anger and Children's Socioemotional Development: Can Parenting Elicit a Positive Side to a Negative Emotion?" *Journal of Child and Family Studies* 21(5): 845–856.

Rhee, Soo Hyun, et al. 2013. "Early Concern and Disregard for Others as Predictors of Antisocial Behavior. *Journal of Child Psychology and Psychiatry* 54(2): 157–166.

Roben, Caroline, Pamela Cole, and Laura Marie Armstrong. 2013. "Longitudinal Relations among Language Skills, Anger Expression, and Regulatory Strategies in Early Childhood." *Child Development* 84(3): 891–905.

Rogoff, Barbara, et al. 2003. "Firsthand Learning through Intent Participation." *Annual Review of Psychology* 54: 175–203.

Ross, Hildy, Ori Friedman, and Aimee Field. 2015. "Toddlers Assert and Acknowledge Ownership Rights." *Social Development* 24(2): 341–356.

Roth-Hanania, Ronit, Maayan Davidov, and Carolyn Zahn-Waxler. 2011. "Empathy Development from 8 to 16 Months: Early Signs of Concern for Others." *Infant Behavior and Development* 34(3): 447–458.

Rubin, Kenneth. 1998. "Social and Emotional Development from a Cultural Perspective." *Developmental Psychology* 34(4): 611–615.

Rubin, Kenneth. 2002. *The Friendship Factor*. New York: Penguin Books.

Rubin, Kenneth, and Robert J. Coplan. 2004. "Paying Attention to and Not Neglecting Social Withdrawal and Social Isolation." *Merrill-Palmer Quarterly* 50(4): 506–534.

Rubin, Kenneth, Robert J. Coplan, and Julie C. Bowker. 2009. "Social Withdrawal in Childhood." *Annual Review of Psychology* 60: 141–171.

Rubin, Kenneth, Amy K. Root, and Julie C. Bowker. 2010. "Parents, Peers, and Social Withdrawal in Childhood: A Relationship Perspective." *New Directions for Child and Adolescent Development* 127: 79–94.

Ryalls Brigette, Robina Gul, and Kenneth Ryalls. 2000. "Infant Imitation of Peer and Adult Models: Evidence for a Peer Model Advantage." *Merrill Palmer Quarterly* 46(1): 188–202.

Sanefuji, Wakako, Hidehiro Ohgami, and Kazuhide Hashiya. 2006. "Preference for Peers in Infancy." *Infant Behavior and Development* 29(4): 584–593.

Schechter, Daniel S., Susan Coates, and Elsa First. 2002. "Observations of Acute Reactions of Young Children and Their Families to the World Trade Center Attacks." *Bulletin of Zero to Three: National Center for Infants, Toddlers, and Families* 22(3): 9–13.

Scola, Celine, Claire Holvoet, Thomas Arciszewski, and Delphine Picard. 2015. "Further Evidence for Infants' Preference for Prosocial over Antisocial Behaviors." *Infancy* 20(6): 684–692.

Sebastián-Enesco, Carla, Maria V. Hernández-Lloreda, and Fernando Colmenares. 2013. "Two-and-a- Half-Year-Old Children Are Prosocial Even When Their Partners Are Not." *Journal of Experimental Child Psychology* 116(2): 186–198.

Séguin, Jean R., Sophie Parent, Richard E. Tremblay, and Phillip David Zelazo. 2009. "Different Neurocognitive Functions Regulating Physical Aggression and Hyperactivity in Early Childhood." *Journal of Child Psychology and Psychiatry* 50(6): 679–687.

Selby, Jane, and Benjamin Bradley. 2003. "Infants in Groups: A Paradigm for the Study of Early Social Experience." *Human Development* 46(4): 197–221.

Shantz, Caroline U. 1987. "Conflicts between Children." *Child Development* 58(2): 283–305.

Shin, Minsun. 2010. "Peeking at the Relationship World of Infant Friends and Caregivers." *Journal of Early Childhood Research* 8(3): 294–302.

Shin, Minsun. 2012. "The Role of Joint Attention in Social Communication and Play among Infants." *Journal of Early Childhood Research* 10(3): 309–317.

Shin, Minsun. 2015. "Enacting Caring Pedagogy in the Infant Classroom." *Early Child Development and Care* 185(3): 496–508.

Shonkoff, Jack, and Deborah Phillips, eds. 2000. *From Neurons to Neighborhoods: The Science of Early Childhood Development*. Washington, DC: National Academy Press.

Sims, Margaret, Andrew Guilfoyle, and Trevor Parry. 2006. "Children's Cortisol Levels and Quality of Child Care Provision." *Child: Care, Health and Development* 32(4): 453–466.

Singer, Elly, and Maritta Hännikäinen. 2002. "The Teacher's Role in Territorial Conflicts of 2- to 3-Year-Old Children. *Journal of Research in Childhood Education* 17(1): 5–18.

Singer, Elly, Anne-Greth Van Hoogdalem, Dorian De Haan, and Nienke Bekkema. 2012. "Daycare Experiences and the Development of Conflict Strategies in Young Children." *Early Child Development and Care* 182(12): 1661–1672.

Solnit, A. J. 2002. "Supporting Parents, Helping Children: Some Questions and Principles." *Zero to Three* 22(3): 16–17.

Sommerville, Jessica, Marco F. H. Schmidt, Jung-eun Yun, and Monica Burns. 2013. "The Development of Fairness Expectations and Prosocial Behavior in the Second Year of Life." *Infancy* 18(1): 40–66.

Spinrad, Tracy L., and Cynthia A. Stifter. 2006. "Toddlers' Empathy-Related Responding to Distress: Predictions from Negative Emotionality and Maternal Behavior in Infancy." *Infancy* 10(2): 97–121.

Strayer, Janet, and William Roberts. 2004. "Children's Anger, Emotional Expressiveness, and Empathy: Relations with Parents' Empathy, Emotional Expressiveness, and Parenting Practices." *Social Development* 13(2): 229–254.

Stupica, Brandi, Laura J. Sherman, and Jude Cassidy. 2011. "Newborn Irritability Moderates the Association between Infant Attachment Security and Toddler Exploration and Sociability." *Child Development* 82(5): 1381–1389.

Svetlova, Margarita, Sara Nichols, and Celia Brownell. 2010. "Toddlers' Prosocial Behavior: From Instrumental to Empathic to Altruistic Helping." *Child Development* 81(6): 1814–1827.

Tailor, Ketan, and Nicole Letourneau. 2012. "Infants Exposed to Intimate Partner Violence: Issues of Gender and Sex." *Journal of Family Violence* 27(5): 477–488.

Teicher, Martin H., and Jacqueline A. Samson. 2016. "Annual Research Review: Enduring Neurobiological Effects of Childhood Abuse and Neglect." *Journal of Child Psychology and Psychiatry* 57(3): 241–266.

Theilheimer, Rachel. 2006. "Molding to the Children: Primary Caregiving and Continuity of Care." *Zero to Three* 26(3): 50–54.

Thompson, Ross A., and Emily K. Newton. 2013. "Baby Altruists? Examining the Complexity of Prosocial Motivation in Young Children." *Infancy* 18(1): 120–133.

Thornberg, Robert. 2006. "The Situated Nature of Preschool Children's Conflict Strategies." *Educational Psychology* 26(1): 109–126.

Todd, Brenda K., John A. Barry, and Sara A. O. Thommessen. 2016. "Preferences for 'Gender-Typed' Toys in Boys and Girls Aged 9 to 32 Months." *Infant and Child Development*. http://www.pitt.edu/~bertsch/Todd_et_al-2016-Infant_and_Child_Development.pdf

Tremblay, Richard. 2004. "Decade of Behavior Distinguished Lecture: Development of Physical Aggression during Infancy." *Infant Mental Health Journal* 25(5): 399–407.

Trevarthen, Colwyn. 2001. "Intrinsic Motives for Companionship in Understanding: Their Origin, Development, and Significance for Infant Mental Health." *Infant Mental Health Journal* 22(1): 95–131.

Trevarthen, Colwyn, and Kenneth J. Aitken. 2001. "Infant Intersubjectivity: Research, Theory, and Clinical Applications." *Journal of Child Psychology and Psychiatry* 42(1): 3–48.

Ulber, Julia, Katharina Hamann, and Michael Tomasello. 2015. "How 18- and 24-Month-Old Peers Divide Resources among Themselves." *Journal of Experimental Child Psychology* 140: 228–244.

Vaillant-Molina, Mariana, Lorraine Bahrick, and Ross Flom. 2013. "Young Infants Match Facial and Vocal Emotional Expressions of Other Infants." *Infancy* 18(s1): E97–E111.

Vaish Amrisha, Malinda Carpenter, and Michael Tomasello. 2010. "Young Children Selectively Avoid Helping People with Harmful Intentions." *Child Development* 81(6): 1661–1669.

Vallotton, Claire, and Catherine Ayoub. 2011. "Use Your Words: The Role of Language in the Development of Toddlers' Self-Regulation." *Early Childhood Research Quarterly* 26(2): 169–181.

Van Hecke, Amy Vaughan, et al. 2007. "Infant Joint Attention, Temperament, and Social Competence in Preschool Children." *Child Development* 78(1): 53–69.

Vaughn, Brian E., et al. 2003. "Negative Interactions and Social Competence for Preschool Children in Two Samples: Reconsidering the Interpretation of Aggressive Behavior for Young Children." *Merrill-Palmer Quarterly* 49(3): 245–278.

Vygotsky, Lev. 1978. *Mind in Society: The Development of Higher Psychological Processes*. Cambridge, MA: Harvard University Press.

Vygotsky, Lev. 1987. "Thinking and Speech." In *The Collected Works of L. S. Vygotsky, Vol. 1: Problems in General Psychology*. New York: Plenum.

Waller, Rebecca, Daniel S. Shaw, Erika E. Forbes, and Luke W. Hyde. 2015. "Understanding Early Contextual and Parental Risk Factors for the Development of Limited Prosocial Emotions." *Journal of Abnormal Child Psychology* 43(6): 1025–1039.

Warneken, Felix. 2013. "Young Children Proactively Remedy Unnoticed Accidents." *Cognition* 126(1): 101–108.

Warneken, Felix, and Michael Tomasello. 2007. "Helping and Cooperation at 14 Months of Age." *Infancy* 11(3): 271–294.

Warneken, Felix, and Michael Tomasello. 2008. "Extrinsic Rewards Undermine Altruistic Tendencies in 20-Month-Olds. *Developmental Psychology* 44(6): 1785–1788.

Watamura, Sarah, Bonny Donzella, Jan Alwin, and Megan Gunnar. 2003. "Morning-to-Afternoon Increases in Cortisol Concentrations for Infants and Toddlers at Child Care: Age Differences and Behavioral Correlates." *Child Development* 74(4): 1006–1020.

Watamura, Sarah, Erin Kryzer, and Steven Robertson. 2009. "Cortisol Patterns at Home and Child Care: Afternoon Differences and Evening Recovery in Children Attending Very High Quality Full-Day Center-Based Child Care." *Journal of Applied Developmental Psychology* 30(4): 475–485.

Weisleder, Adriana, and Anne Fernald. 2013. "Talking to Children Matters: Early Language Experience Strengthens Processing and Builds Vocabulary." *Psychological Science* 24(11): 2143–2152.

Whaley, Kimberlee, and Tamera Rubenstein. 1994. "How Toddlers 'Do' Friendship: A Descriptive Analysis of Naturally Occurring Friendships in a Group Child Care Setting." *Journal of Social and Personal Relationship* 11(3): 383–400.

Wiggins, Crystal, Emily Fenichel, and Tammy Mann. 2007. "Literature Review: Developmental Problems of Maltreated Children and Early Intervention Options for Maltreated Children." http://aspe.hhs.gov/hsp/07/Children-CPS/litrev/report.pdf

Williams, Shannon, Lenna Ontai, and Ann Mastergeorge. 2007. "Reformulating Infant and Toddler Social Competence with Peers." *Infant Behavior and Development* 30(2): 353–365.

Williamson, Rebecca A., Meghan R. Donohue, and Erin C. Tully. 2013. "Learning How to Help Others: Two-Year-Olds' Social Learning of a Prosocial Act." *Journal of Experimental Child Psychology* 114(4): 543–550.

Wittmer, Donna S., and Sandra H. Petersen. 2017. *Infant and Toddler Development and Responsive Program Planning: A Relationship-Based Approach*. Upper Saddle River, NJ: Pearson/Prentice Hall.

Zahn-Waxler, Carolyn, Barbara Hollenbeck, and Marian Radke-Yarrow. 1984. "The Origins of Empathy and Altruism." In *Advances in Animal Welfare Science* 1984/85. Washington, DC: Humane Society of the United States.

Zahn-Waxler, Carolyn , Marian Radke-Yarrow, and Robert King. 1979. "Child Rearing and Children's Prosocial Initiations toward Victims of Distress." *Child Development* 50(2): 319–330.

Zahn-Waxler, Carolyn, Marian Radke-Yarrow, Elizabeth Wagner, and Michael Chapman. 1992. "Development of Concern for Others." *Developmental Psychology* 28(1): 126–136.

Zero to Three. 2016. "National Parent Survey: Overview and Key Insights." Zero to Three. https://www.zerotothree.org/resources/1424-national-parent-survey-overview-and-key-insights

Zmyj, Norbert, Gisa Aschersleben, Wolfgang Prinz, and Moritz Daum. 2012. "The Peer Model Advantage in Infants' Imitation of Familiar Gestures Performed by Differently Aged Models." *Frontiers in Psychology* 3: 252.

Zmyj, Norbert, and Sabine Seehagen. 2013. "The Role of a Model's Age for Young Children's Imitation: A Research Review." *Infant and Child Development* 22(6): 622–641.

Index

I

Identifying emotions, 3, 14–15, 45, 54, 61, 63, 70, 77, 83, 123, 141, 145, 151–152
- conflict resolution, 110–111, 115
- infants, 29, 37
- peer conflicts, 88–89

Imitating, 8–9, 22, 23, 26, 41, 44, 51, 60, 66, 160
- biting, 120–122, 140–141
- deferred, 122
- young toddlers, 32–33, 38

Inclusion, 41

Inconsistent caregiving, 11–12

Infants, 3, 68
- caring capacity, 55
- communication, 29–30
- conflicts in, 91–92, 97
- detecting emotions, 29
- developing social skills, 28–30, 37
- distinguishing self from others, 28–29
- empathy, 68
- identifying emotions, 37
- initiating interactions, 29-30, 37
- making social judgments, 57, 68, 157-159
- peer behavior, 158–159
- prosocial development, 57–59, 68
- sharing, 78

Inhibited children, 130–132
- strategies to help, 147–148

Initiating peer interaction, 74, 159
- biting, 120–121, 140–141
- infants, 29, 37
- young toddlers, 31–32, 38

Insecure attachment, 17, 137
- influence on conflict, 99

Instrumental help, 60

Interrupted activity, 91, 159–162
- biting, 121
- infants, 92, 97, 103
- toddlers, 94–95, 97–98, 103

Iron deficiency, 126, 143, 150

Isolation, 16, 31, 38

J

Joint attention, 27, 29–30, 38, 159

K

Kicking, 125, 129–130

Kindness, 12, 16–17, 50, 54–55, 57, 71, 76, 161

L

Language deficits, 126, 143, 147, 150, 153
- abuse and neglect, 132

Language skills, 3, 22, 33, 39, 45, 51, 50, 66
- diversity, 41
- older toddlers, 35
- turn taking, 46, 50, 52, 145, 151, 161
- younger toddlers, 33–34

Language-loving adults, 5–6, 50

Lead poisoning, 126, 143, 150

Learning names, 47, 51

Limited prosocial emotions, 128

Lip biting, 131

Listening skills, 15, 34

M

Making social judgments, 158–159
- infants, 57, 68
- toddlers, 60

Mandatory reporting laws, 155

Marital conflict, 128

Mediation strategies, 111–112, 115
- vs. high-power strategies, 111

Memory development, 22

Mind-mindedness, 45, 51, 76

Modeling behaviors, 23, 45–46, 50–51, 63, 76, 78, 82–83, 88–89, 106, 122, 141

N

National Institute of Child Health and Human Development, 18

National Scientific Council on the Developing Child, 5

Neglect, 5, 11–12, 118, 127, 132, 137, 155–156